# Old Grantown to Avi…
# Upper Strathspey

*by* Ann Glen



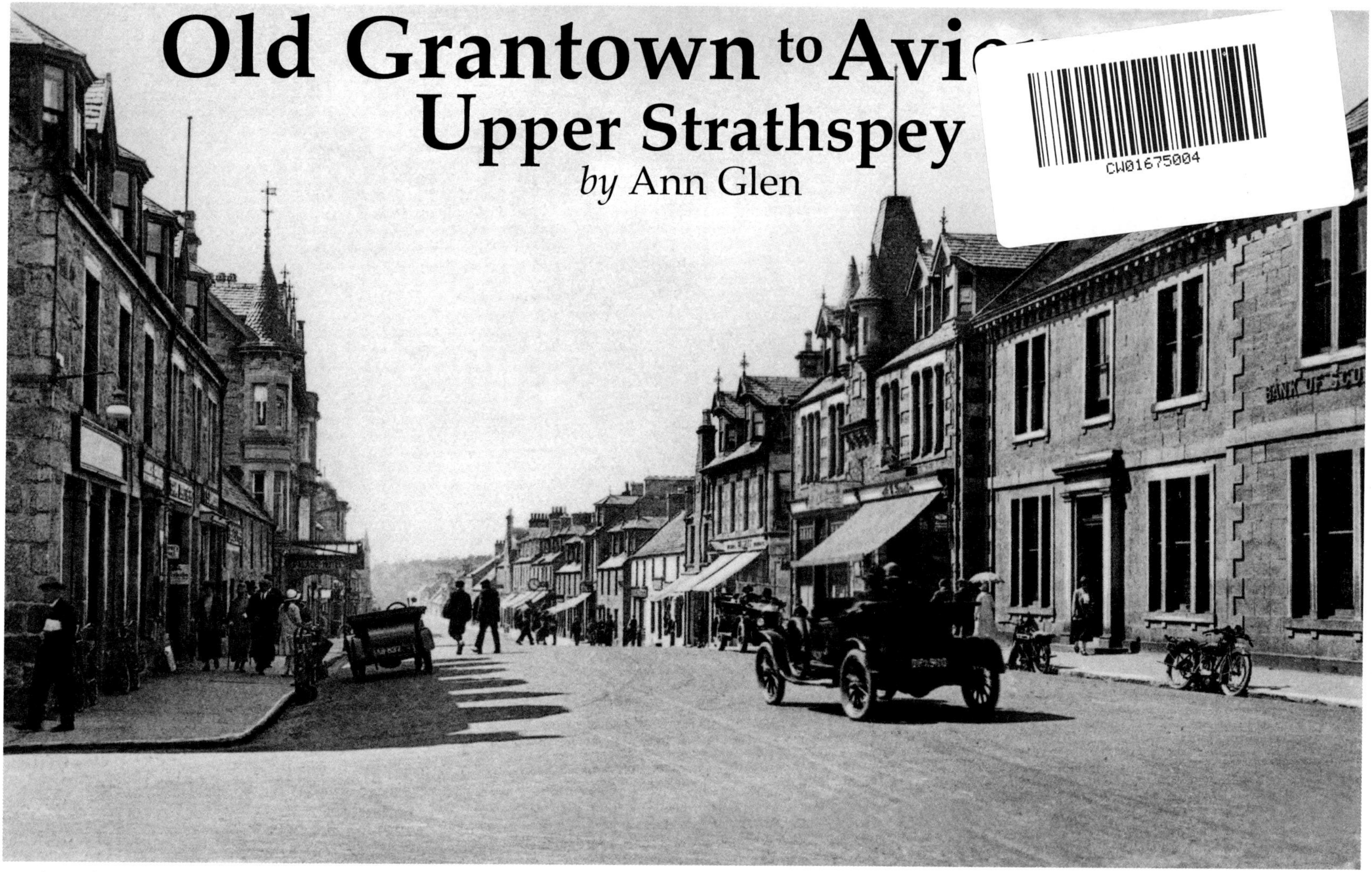

On the right of this 1925 photograph is Grantown's branch of the Bank of Scotland (formerly the Caledonian Bank), built in 1865–67. The turreted building containing the post office also housed the premises of A.C. Grant, supplier of tweeds to His Majesty the King – at the time of this view George V, who came to shooting parties at nearby Tulchan. The imposing building opposite with the cast-iron portico is the Palace Hotel, now a care home.

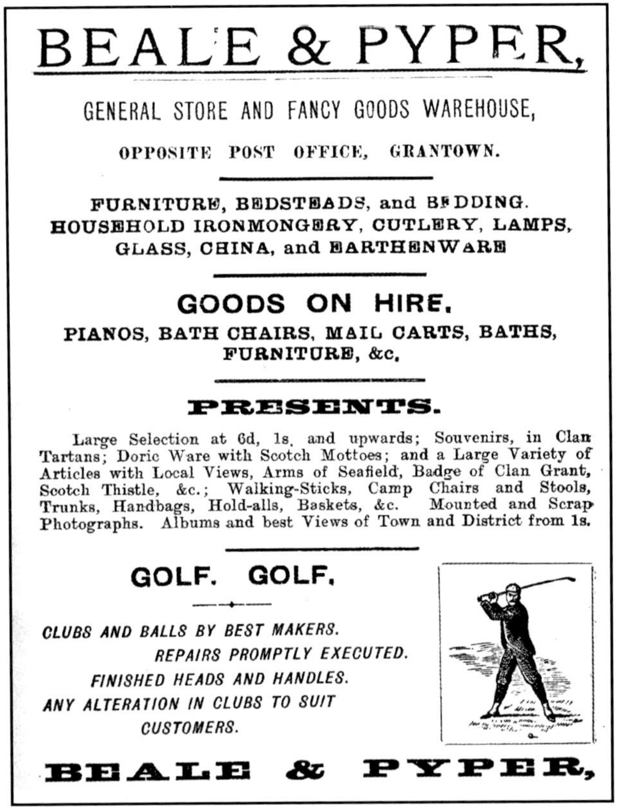


William Shearer Beale and Henry Pyper commenced business as cabinetmakers in Grantown's Woodside Avenue in 1886 and their firm prospered in supplying the many new houses, hotels and shooting lodges in the district. As plumbing arrangements in older properties were basic, they even had baths available for hire. They also specialised in a wide range of souvenirs and supplied golf equipment. By the 1930s they advertised as 'complete house furnishers', providing not only quality furniture and fine china but also acting as auctioneers and valuators from premises in the Square. The name continues, but nowadays on the west side of the High Street.


First published in the United Kingdom, 2009,
reprinted 2011
by Stenlake Publishing Ltd.
www.stenlake.co.uk
ISBN 9781840334593



## Further Reading

The books listed below were used by the author during her research. None of them is available from Stenlake Publishing. Those interested in finding out more are advised to contact their local bookshop or reference library.

W. Forsyth, *In the Shadow of Cairngorm*, Inverness, 1900.
Ann Glen, *The Cairngorm Gateway*, Scottish Cultural Press, 2002.
Elizabeth Grant, *Abernethy Forest, Its People and its Past*, Arkelton Trust, Nethybridge, 1994.
E. Grant, *Memoirs of a Highland Lady*, Canongate, 1997.
A.R.B. Haldane, *New Ways through the Glens*, Nelson, 1962.
O.S. Nock, *The Highland Railway*, Ian Allan, 1965.
H.A. Vallance, *The Great North of Scotland Railway*, David & Charles, 1965.
W. Taylor, *The Military Roads of Scotland*, House of Lochar, 1996.
A. Wightman, *Who Owns Scotland*, Canongate, 1996.

The Statistical Accounts of Scotland (1791–99 and 1834–45) were consulted, as were the Valuation Rolls for Elginshire and Inverness-shire. Use was also made of heritors' records, estate papers and newspaper files.

## Acknowledgements

The author wishes to thank the following for sharing their knowledge and information: George A. Dixon, the well known expert on the history of the Seafield estate; Walter Dempster; Richard Eccles; Alastair McCook; Rita Templeton; James Richard; Colin Riddell; and Paul Mackay, Secretary of Grantown-on-Spey Golf Club. The staff at the Royal Archives, Windsor Castle, Highland Council Archives, Moray Council Archives and the National Archives of Scotland are also thanked for their assistance. Molly Duckett of Grantown Museum has kindly provided the photographs on pages 2 and 16 and David Rose of the Badenoch & Strathspey Local History Group has kindly made available the photograph on page 29. John Peter has prepared all the photographs for publication.

The publishers wish to thank the author for contributing the photographs on the front cover, the inside front cover, pages 1, 4, 7, 17 top, 23, 32, 38 right, 45 (both) and 48, the inside back cover and the back cover.

# Introduction

Strathspey is a great natural corridor stretching from the margin of the Grampian Mountains towards the Moray coast. The upper valley of the River Spey is reckoned to begin at Aviemore and extends to Cromdale where the Highland Council boundary lies. The river confers both character and unity on the area it flows through. Northward its waters are augmented by the Druie, the Nethy, the Dulnain and other streams. The high Cairngorms rise on the south and east while the Monadhliath range and outliers – the Kincardine Hills, the Braes of Abernethy and the Cromdale Hills – add to the diversity of the landscape.

In the twelfth century the ancient Province of Moray was split into 'lordships' and one of these was Strathspey. On behalf of the king, the Bishop of Moray ensured that such territory was controlled by putting approved noblemen or 'thanes' in charge of portions of it. One name is especially associated with Strathspey – it is the country of Clan Grant where the chief and his relations held sway from the fourteenth century. Soon they had a link with Freuchie, close to the site of Grantown. In 1493 their land became a barony and a castle arose with a hamlet, known as Ballachastle (Baile a'Chaisteil, the 'township of the castle'), beside it. Gradually, Grant territory, at one time described as 'ane great Hudge Estait', covered much of Strathspey. On its southern edge stood Craigellachie, the 'rock of the alarm', the clan's beacon hill in time of trouble.

Close by was Rothiemurchus and in 1570 the chief secured it for his second son, Patrick of Muckerach, strengthening Grant identity. Eastwards, Glenmore was once a royal forest but in 1685 it became a possession of the Gordons. As Earls of Huntly (and later Dukes of Gordon) they dominated an immense tract from Ben Avon to Lochaber and, unlike the Grants, they were pro-Jacobite and Royalist. Kincardine, lying east of the Spey, was territory of the Stewarts who had similar sympathies.

Clan chiefs had heritable jurisdictions, or the right to administer justice, and they exercised the king's rights for him as sheriffs, punishing wrongdoers at 'Baron Baillie' courts. In 1663 the lands of Strathspey received extra status as a Barony of Regality. The chiefs could call out clansmen for military service and could also regulate trade. The wealth of the clan lay in its herds of cattle and its strength in its manpower.

In 1690 the Civil War saw 600 men from Clan Grant augment General Mackay's troops at the battle of Cromdale when opposing Highlanders on the Royalist side were routed. After the Jacobite rising of 1715 the chief supplied men for an Independent Highland Company, a type of Home Guard, from which the Black Watch Regiment can trace its descent. Their purpose was to maintain order and prevent cattle rustling.

By 1725 General Wade's troops were building roads to link up fortresses and a key route went through part of Strathspey, making for Inverness. Although the intention was subjugation, these roads opened up the country and inns appeared to serve the military, administrators and ordinary travellers. At Aviemore, where a track from the castle at Freuchie joined the King's Highway, a basic inn with a thatched roof was an initiative by the Chief of Grant. During the 1745 rising the Grants were ambivalent – the chief was loyal to the Hanoverian government while the clansmen were less convinced and took part only to a limited extent as individuals. Subsequently, the Highland chiefs' power was curtailed and so wealth, titles and government positions took precedence over their hereditary rights and responsibilities within the clan.

By the 1760s there was a new chief, James Grant of Grant, who was an exponent of land reorganisation, forestry, planned settlements and industry. His estate was surveyed with a view to making it more productive and the new village of Grantown was established. His concern for his people's welfare showed in his attempts to relieve famine by distributing grain and in the establishment of the Speyside Charity School, the first orphanage in the Highlands.

The early nineteenth century saw hardship return with emigration at worrying levels. However, the growing interest in sporting estates from the 1830s onwards brought a surge in income, first to landowners and then to rates levied on properties, later including railways, in the Highland counties. By the 1880s many shooting lodges had been built, attracting mainly aristocrats or those with 'new money' earned in industry and trade.

The completion of the Inverness & Perth Junction Railway in 1863, soon to become the Highland Railway, brought in many middle-class visitors. This had a profound effect on Grantown. Already a service focus with banks, insurance offices, a courthouse and 16 fairs a year, it now grew as a resort with hotels, boarding houses and villas for let. It boasted a good water supply, a gas light company, and became a burgh in 1898.

At the other extremity, Aviemore had only its rebuilt inn of the 1760s and a few cottages, but it also benefited from the railway, especially when it became a junction in the 1890s. As the nearest village to the Cairngorms, it was bound to grow. The appeal of the strath's villages for family holidays was increased by adding facilities for golf and tennis.

The interwar years saw the rise of car tourism and in the 1960s a winter sports boom resulted in profound changes to holidaymaking in Strathspey. Second homes and timeshares, caravan parks and chalets made their appearance. Much of the old Grant lands of the Seafield estate were split up and sold off, including Castle Grant itself. Only portions of the estate were retained but the Grants of Rothiemurchus still hold on to their 'duchus' or homeland. The Cairngorms National Park, the Forestry Commission and the Royal Society for the Protection of Birds now assume aspects of the roles of lairds of former times.

In recent years there has been a growing interest in local history with Grantown Heritage Museum, Nethybridge Heritage Centre, and other groups in action. To reinforce their identities, villages have been branding themselves. There is a resurgence in local traditions, such as Grantown's Figget Fair, in shinty and in Gaelic as people take a renewed interest in both their ancestry and place.

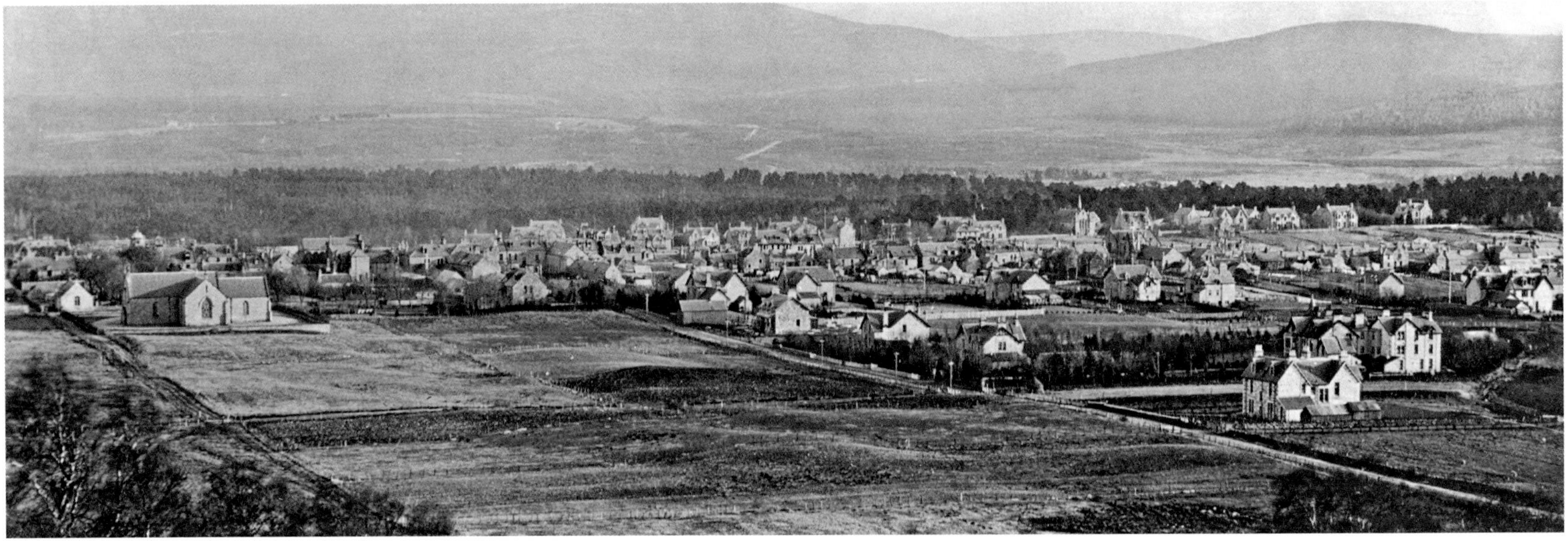

In 1766 the planned village of Grantown was begun by James Grant of Grant. It was to have an industrial focus, but the manufacturing of stockings, weaving and other trades were not successful and it became a service centre for the district. By 1841 it had a population of 1,000. After the Inverness & Perth Junction Railway opened in 1863, the town's popularity as a holiday resort grew and soon there were two stations, 'West ' and 'East', serving 'Grantown-on-Spey'. This view towards Grantown's core in the early 1900s shows the remodelled Free Church on Woodside Avenue (far left) and villa developments. The changing pattern of holidaymaking has often led to their conversion to hotels and guesthouses.

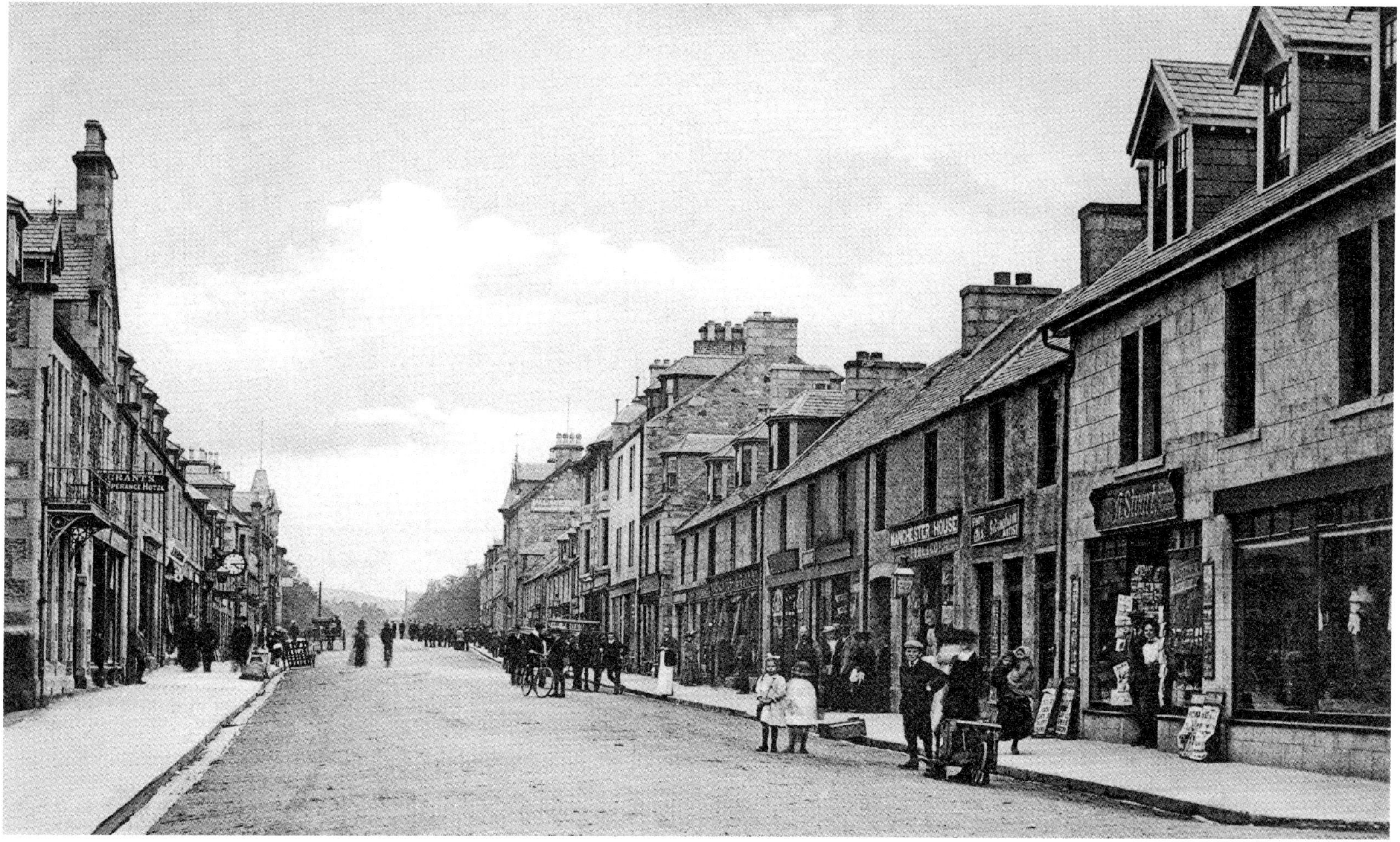


This view, looking north along the west end of Grantown's High Street, towards the Square in the early 1900s, reveals much commercial activity. On the left is Grant's Temperance Hotel (now the Ben Mhor Hotel); every resort had such non-licensed premises in those days. The clock sign advertises Imray's, a watch-making business dating from 1826, while the turreted building beyond belongs to the post office. On the right are Stuart's stationer and newsagent, photographer Alex. Ledingham's studio, Mackenzie's 'Manchester House' which specialised in tartans and knitwear, and several shops selling travelling rugs and tweeds. The building at the far end with the sign board on its gable is Hastilow's Palace Hotel, built in 1894 on the site of the Black Bull Inn.

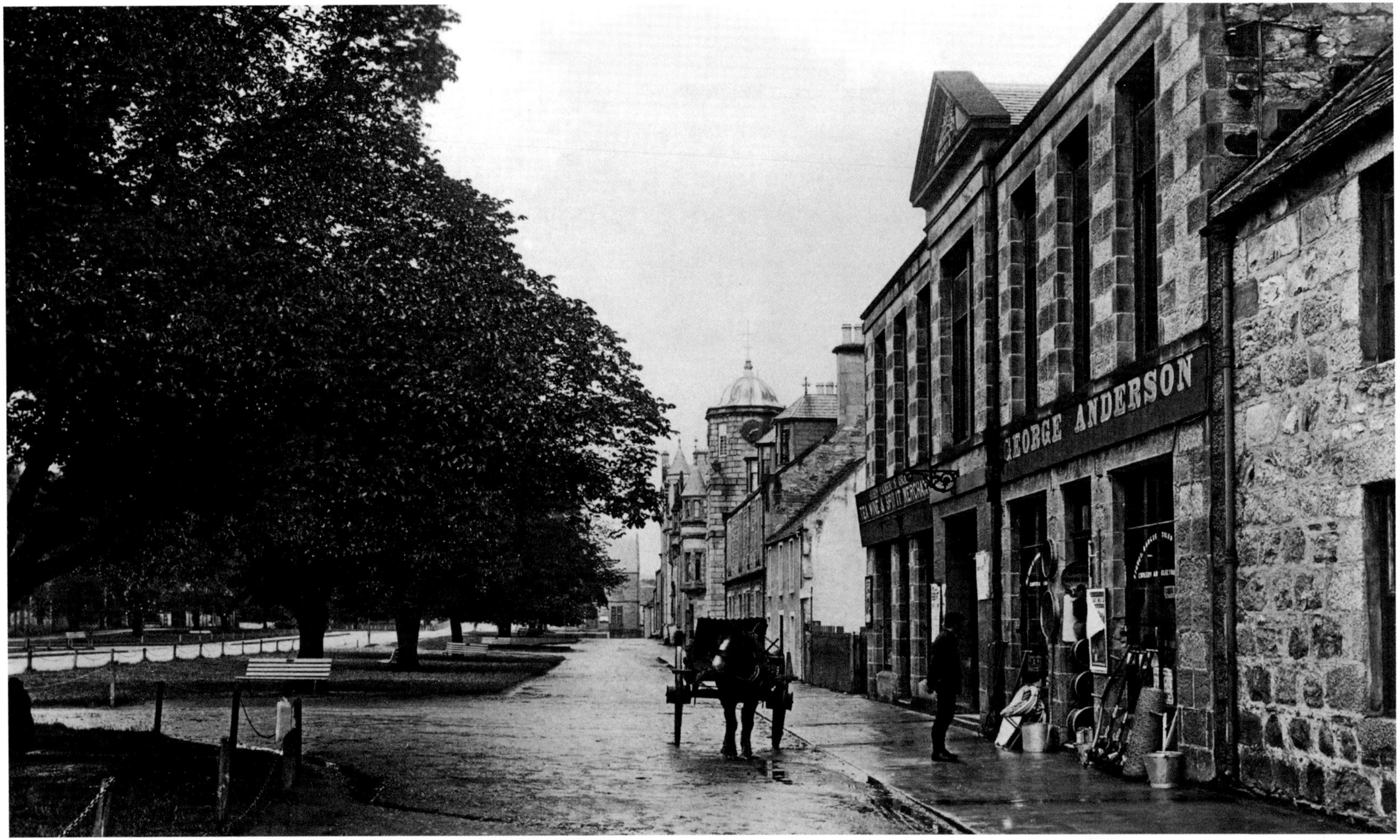


In the early 1900s George Anderson's shop on the east side of Grantown's Square was advertised in local papers as 'The Strathspey Ironmongery and Implement Warehouse', selling stoves and ranges, tiles, cutlery and even electrical goods as there was much house building in progress. Next door is a tea, wine and spirit merchant's shop. On the empty site adjacent a cinema would later be built. The ornamental building with the tower is the Speyside Charity School, erected in 1824 and the first orphanage in the Highlands. It arose from the generosity of the Earl of Seafield, Lady Jane Grant of Monymusk, and Dr Gregory Grant, and continued in local authority use until 1974/75. It has since been converted into private flats.

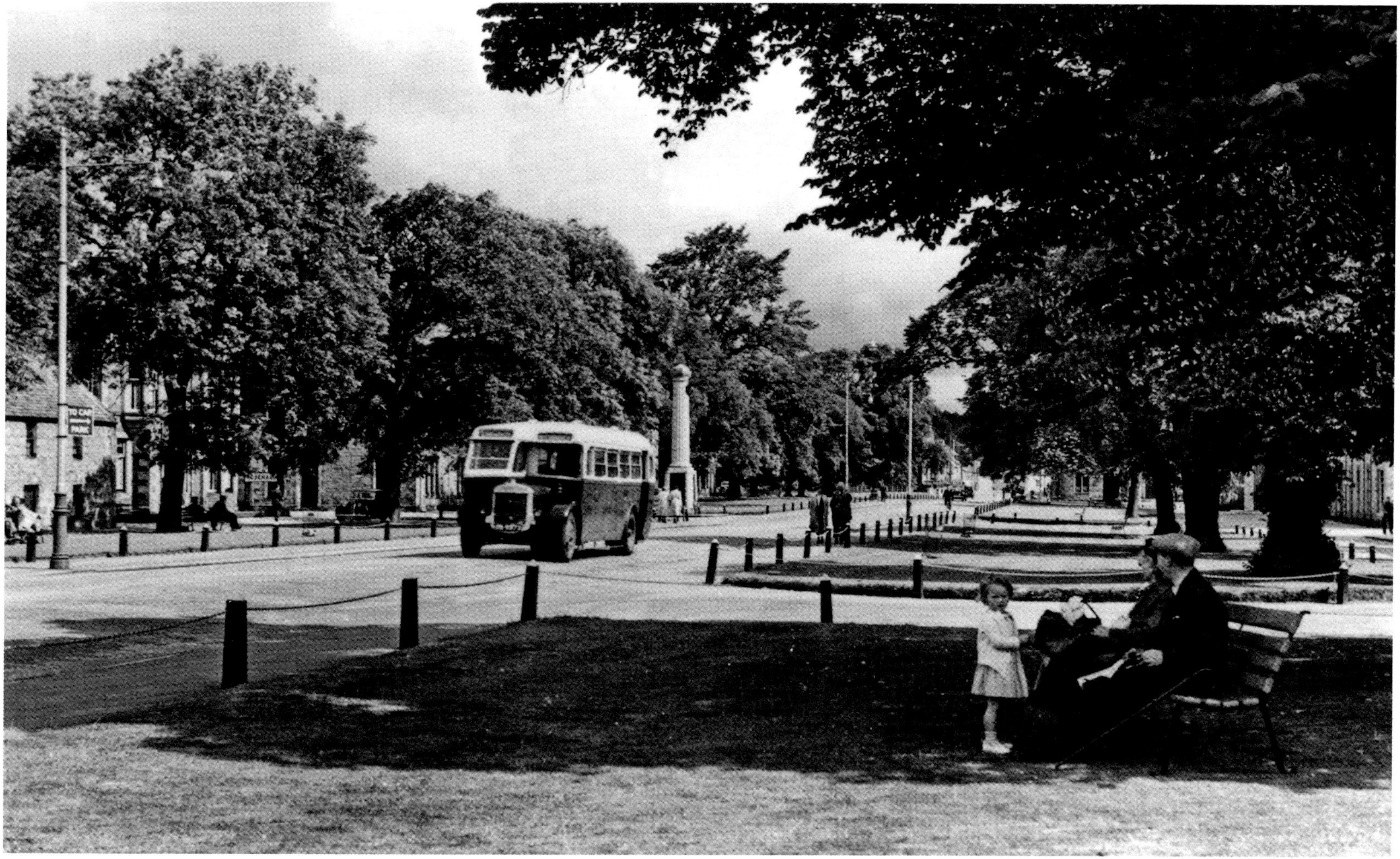


Grantown was built on moorland to a plan devised by the laird, James Grant of Grant. Known as 'Baloor' (Am Baile Ùr – the 'new town'), he advertised 'lots' or parcels of land to manufacturers and tradesmen to settle, and initially encouraged textile manufacture and crafts. At its north end the High Street led into a long tree-lined rectangle known as the Square, making an attractive civic space. By the 1930s Joseph M'Cormack of Kingussie was running his green and cream buses between Newtonmore and Grantown, calling at many places en route. The granite column of the War Memorial (centre) was erected in 1922.

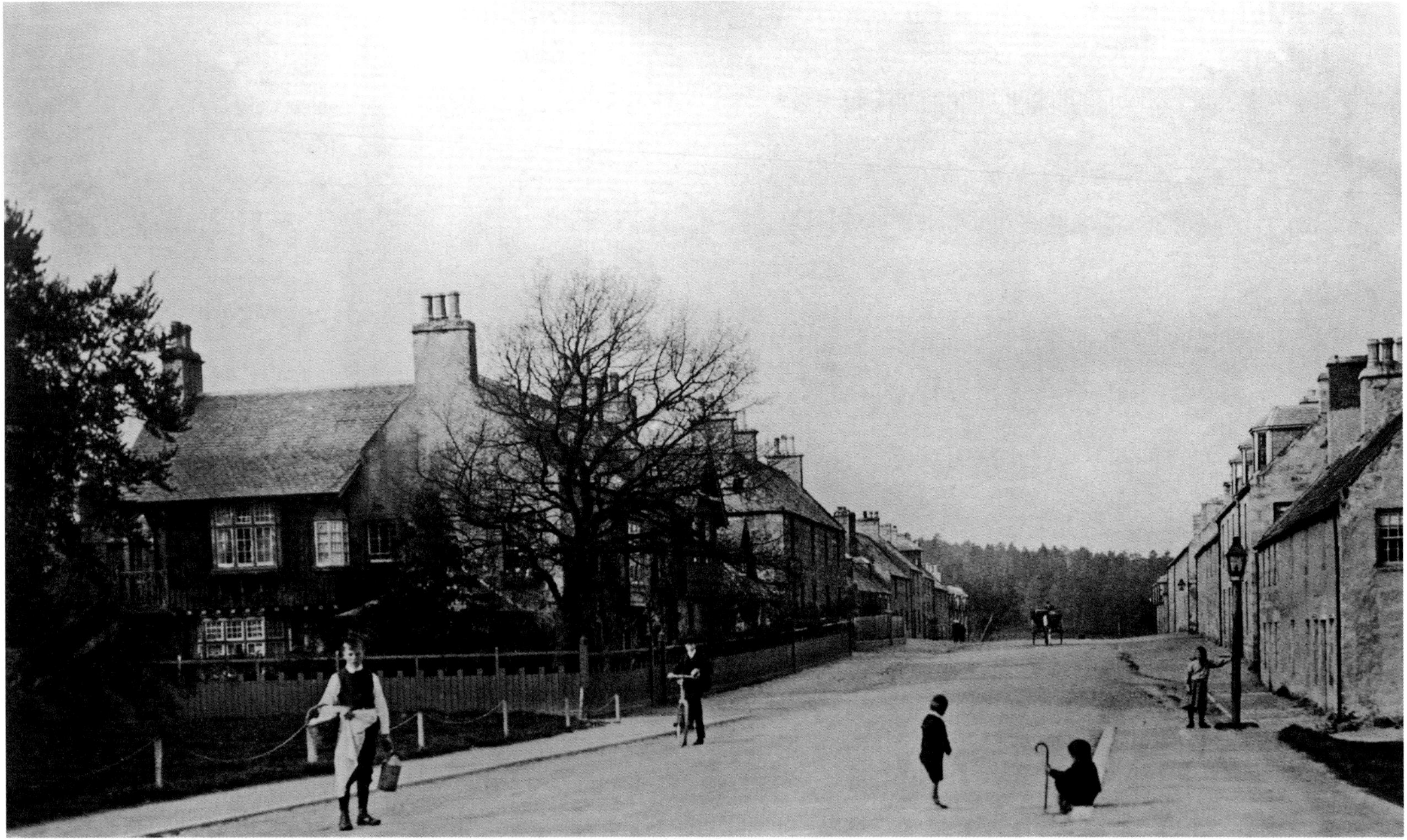

Castle Road at Grantown's East End leads north towards Castle Grant. Part of the building on the left originated in the 1760s, and here James Grant of Grant encouraged a stocking factory employing 42 people although the business failed. Houses with glass windows, where work could be done even in winter, attracted tradesmen to his new town. Few original houses now remain; gone too are the quiet streets of the early 1900s where message boys could walk and children play without fear of traffic. Long ago the old factory became a private house, received 'Arts & Crafts' additions and was converted to the Garth Hotel in the late 1930s.

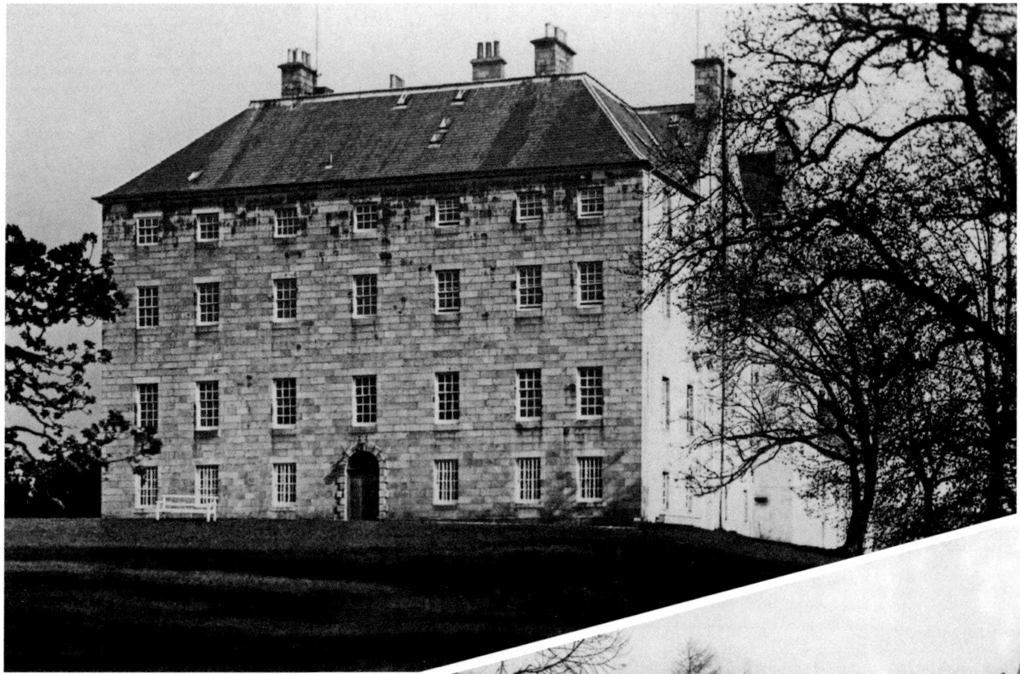

Castle Grant's core is a tall harled range of structures dating from the 1500s. On the north side, this plain addition by John Adam, elder brother of Robert Adam, the classical architect, was constructed of dressed granite in 1753–56. Queen Victoria likened it to a factory when visiting Grantown incognito in 1860. The castle was occupied by the military in the Second World War. Once advertised as 'completely & splendidly furnished and a fit residence for a nobleman's family', it was subsequently stripped of its fine furniture and clan paintings and sold off by the Seafield estate in 1983. It has since had several owners.

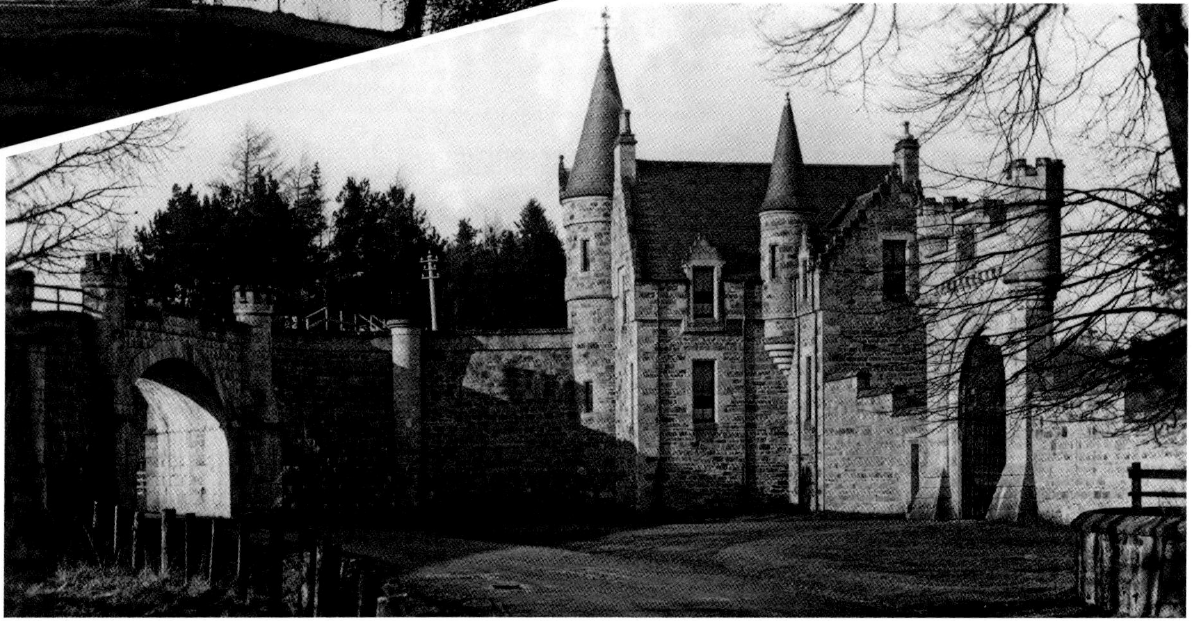

This gatehouse in Gothic Revival style was built in 1864 by the Inverness & Perth Junction Railway for the 7th Earl of Seafield who was a railway enthusiast and a director of the company. The buildings concealed a platform for the Earl's use.

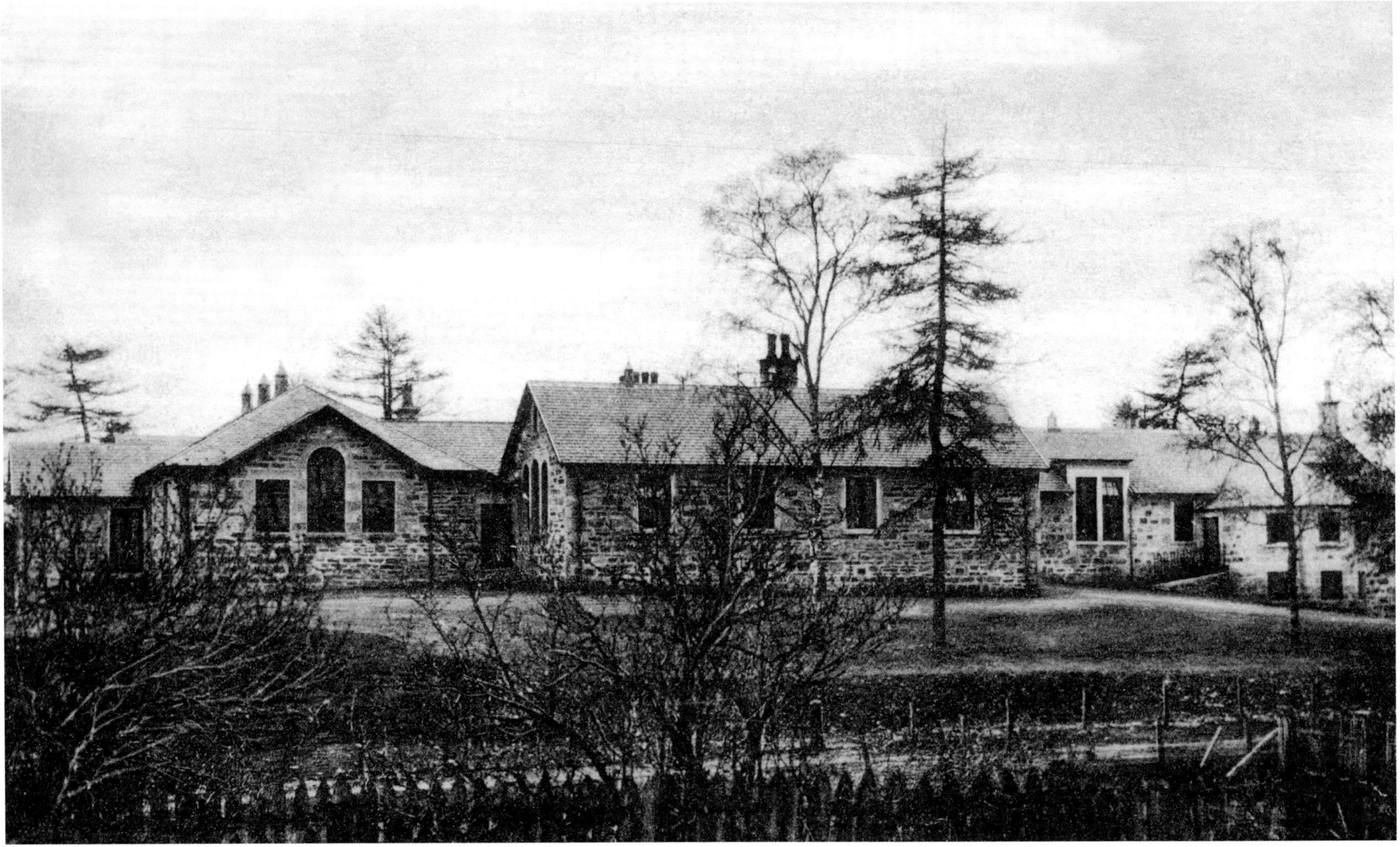

Grammar school education began in Grantown in 1767 when an inn was adapted for the purpose. By the 1840s there were two schools in Grantown – a grammar school and an infant school. Support came from the Earl of Seafield, but parents also had to contribute to teachers' salaries. In 1872 the Education (Scotland) Act introduced compulsory free education; a school board was set up and the premises shown here, combining secondary and primary facilities and with a bell tower, were constructed. Expansion continued and these buildings are now the primary school. As girls were educated separately, the 'boys only' former pupils' club was called 'The Old Guard'.

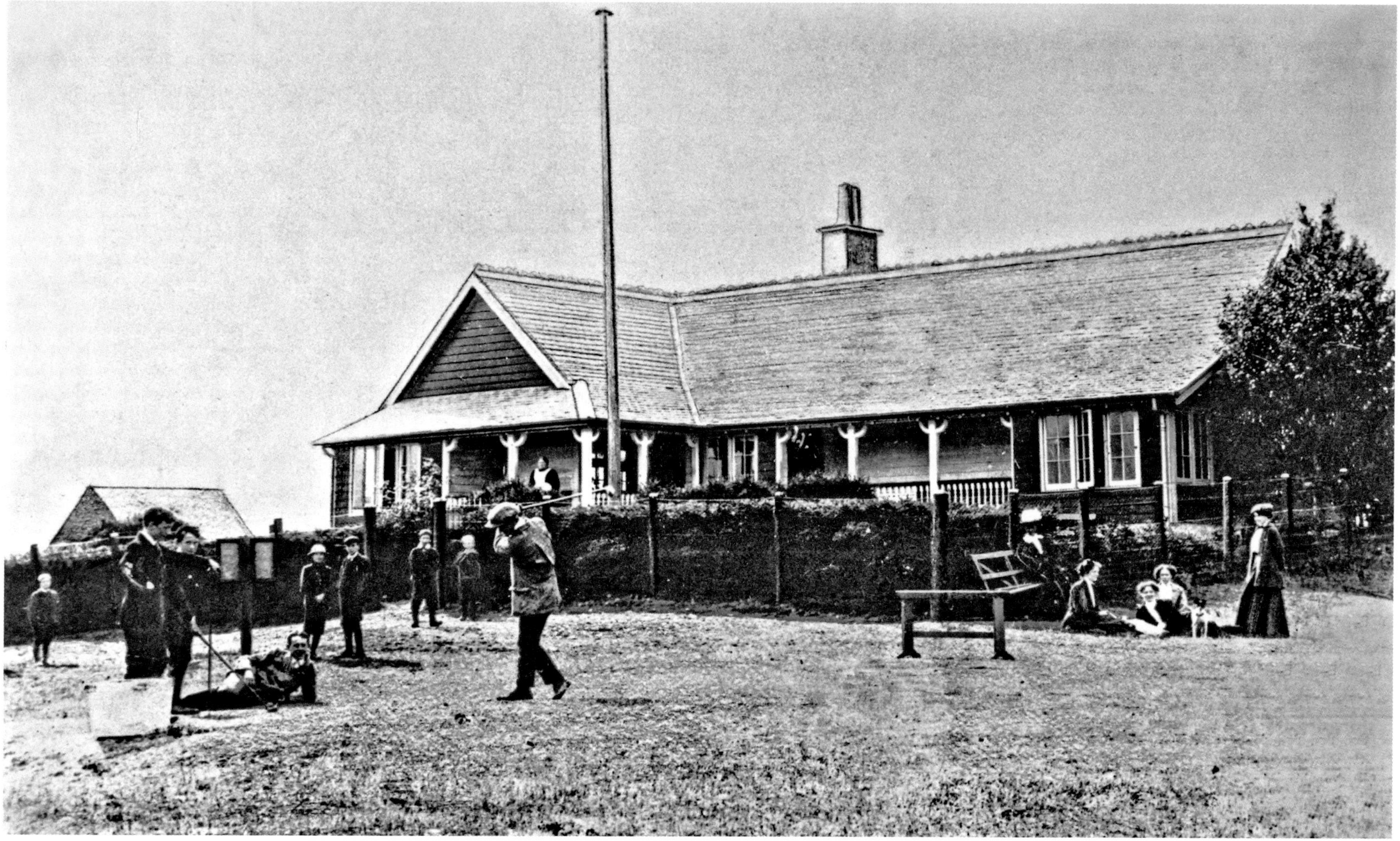

Grantown Golf Course was formed in 1890 with nine holes arranged on park and hilly woodland by A.C. Brown, a professional golfer. In 1911 an extension to 18 holes, designed by former Open Champion Willie Park of Musselburgh, a pioneer of some 170 parkland courses, was completed. A decade later James Braid, the famous Open champion, made further alterations. The club's most distinguished member was Bobby Cruikshank who in 1921 became a professional in the USA, winning more than 20 tournaments there; he was a close friend and rival of Tommy Armour, another Scot who became a great American champion. In 1999 there was major refurbishment of the club pavilion, which dates from the 1890s.

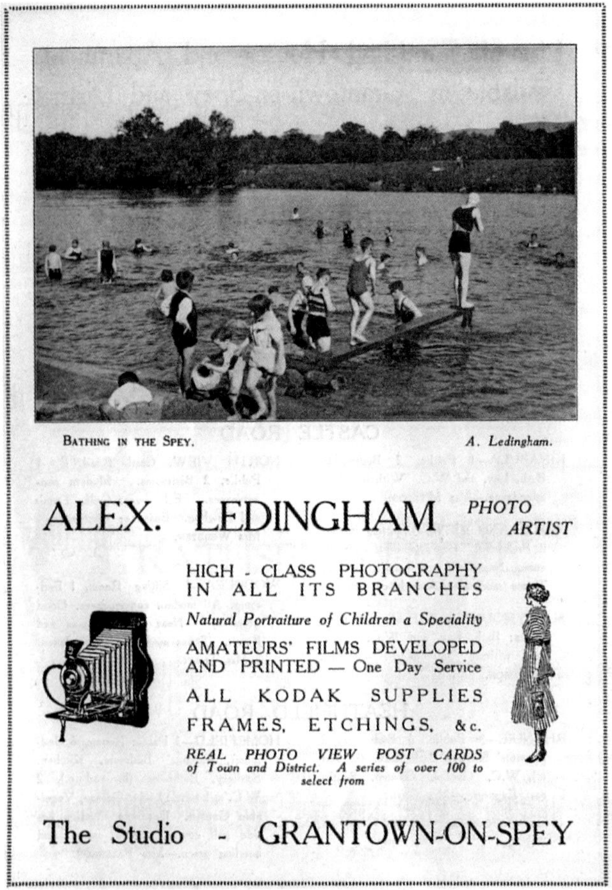


*Left*: Alex. Ledingham was a well-known photographer in Grantown, recording events and views in the district from the early 1900s. He described himself as a 'Photo Artist', producing over 100 postcards of local scenes which are now treasured for their historical value. The photograph in this advertisement from a 1930s guide book to the area shows youngsters swimming from a sandy beach by the River Spey, which flows gently at this point near Grantown. Ledingham also sold Kodak products – the famous 'Kodak Girl' in her striped dress helped to popularise photography among women, although cameras were bulky with leather bellows. They also had slow shutter speeds and spools of film gave only six or eight 'snapshots' per roll.

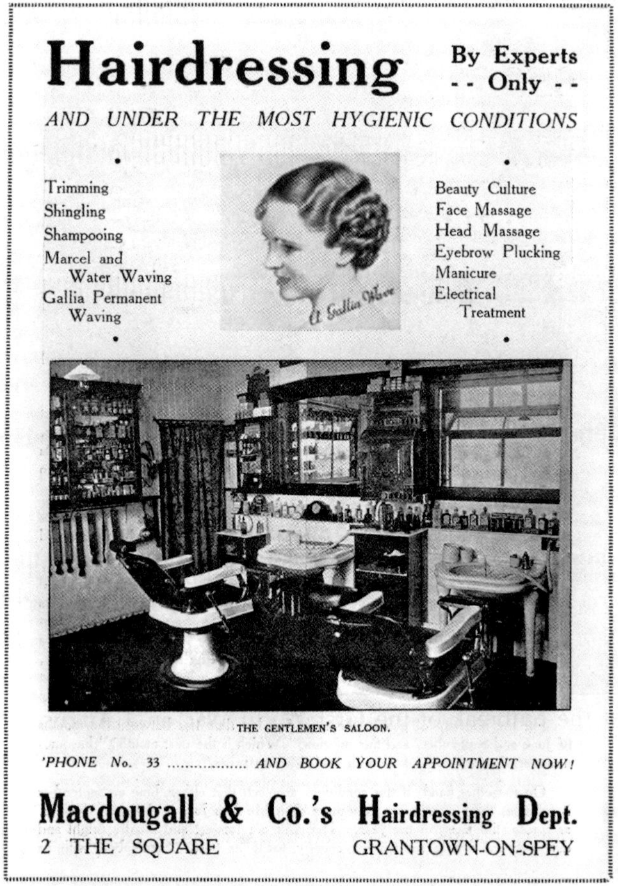


*Right*: In the 1930s Macdougall & Co.'s hairdressing department in the Square at Grantown catered for both male and female customers – in separate salons of course. 'Marcel Waving', a system of using heated rods to put curls and waves in hair, was invented in France in 1875. 'Gallia Permanent Waving', combining chemicals and heat, was pioneered by Karl Nessler in Germany in 1906. Both were risky methods. Long hair went out of fashion in the 1920s and 'shingling', denoting women's emancipation, gave a short bobbed look. Doubtless, the film stars seen on the screen at Grantown's cinema would have been a big influence on styles. Macdougall's also sold a range of goods such as china, sports equipment, luggage, carpets and linoleum.

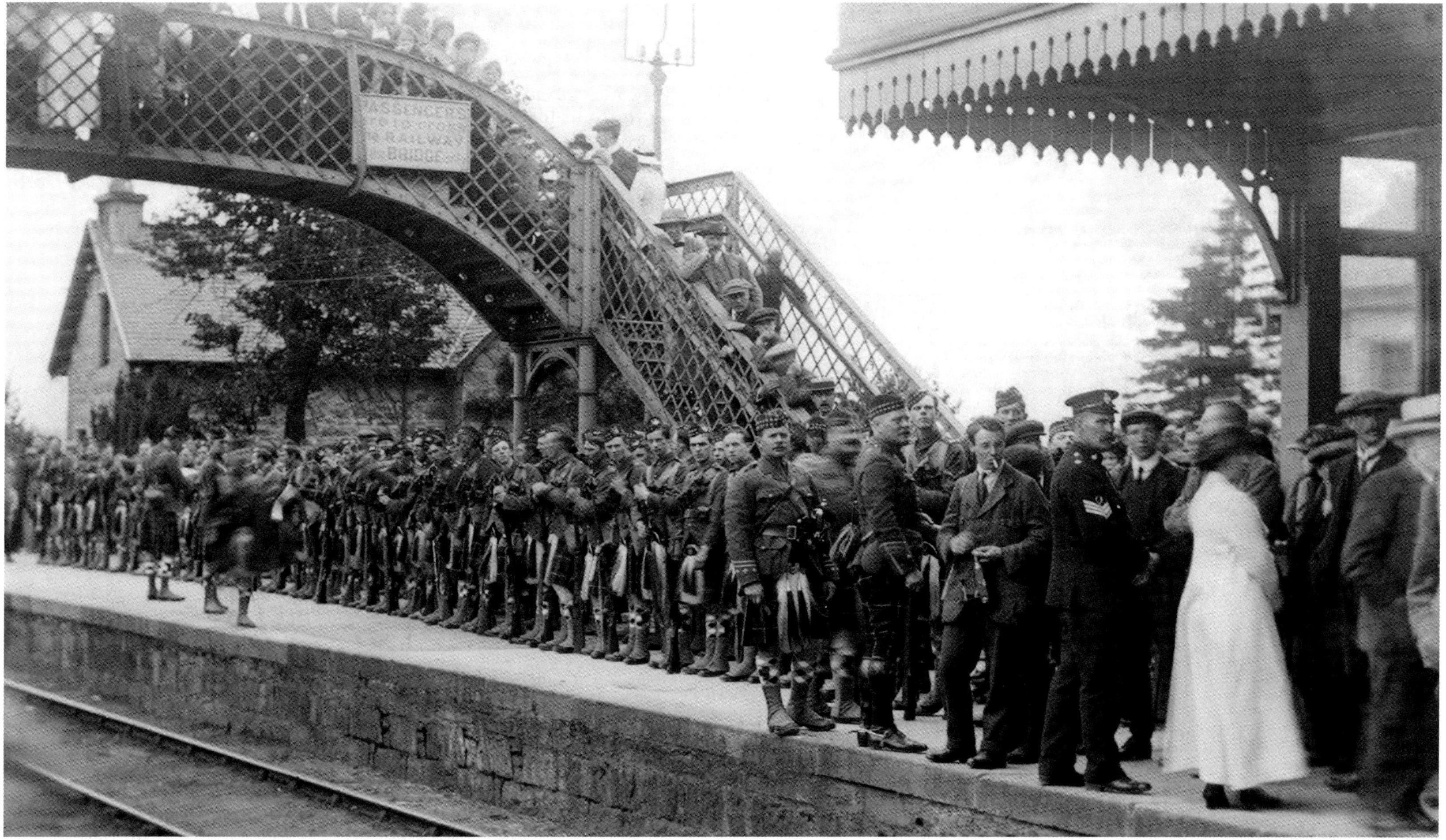


At the outbreak of the First World War on 4 August 1914, territorial battalions of regiments were called to arms. Here, the 6th Battalion Seaforth Highlanders, whose recruiting district was Morayshire, prepare to board a train at Grantown West, at that time one of the town's two stations. This Highland Railway station, on the line from Inverness via Forres, stood to the south of the town and had been rebuilt in 1887 to improve facilities for passengers. Throughout the war the Highland Railway had to make prodigious efforts to cope with increased traffic, both military and naval. By October 1965 both stations were closed to passengers, freight services continued until 1968. The Strathspey Railway intends to reconnect Grantown, via Aviemore, to the Highland main line.

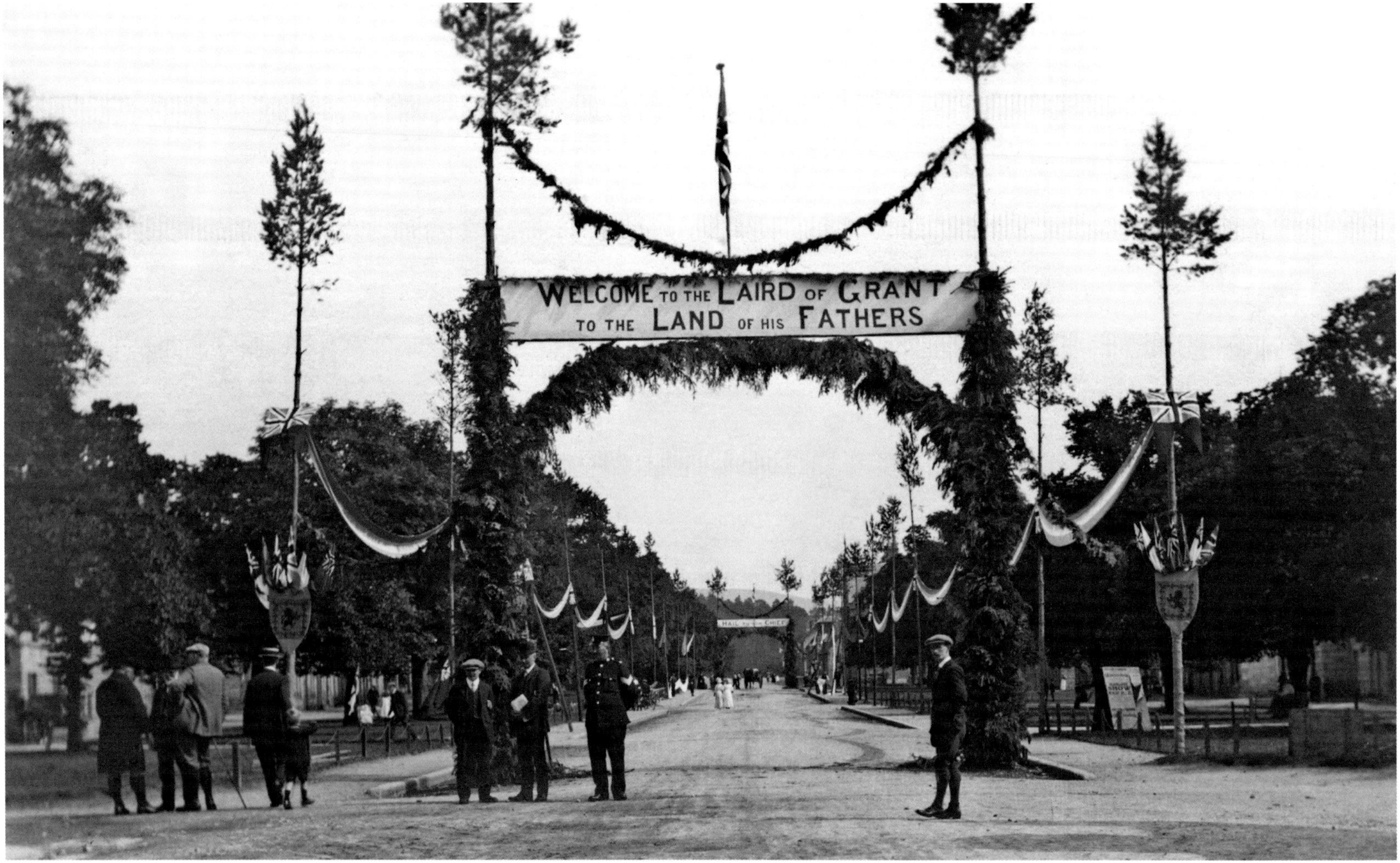


This banner was stretched across the Square in Grantown in July 1912 to welcome James, 11th Earl of Seafield and Chief of Clan Grant on the occasion of his assuming his patrimony. In 1915 he was tragically lost in action in France during the First World War. The Seafield title and estate – one of the largest in Scotland – was inherited by his only child, the nine-year-old Nina, who became Countess of Seafield. However, as a female she could not be clan chief so her uncle therefore became Lord Strathspey and Chief of Clan Grant.

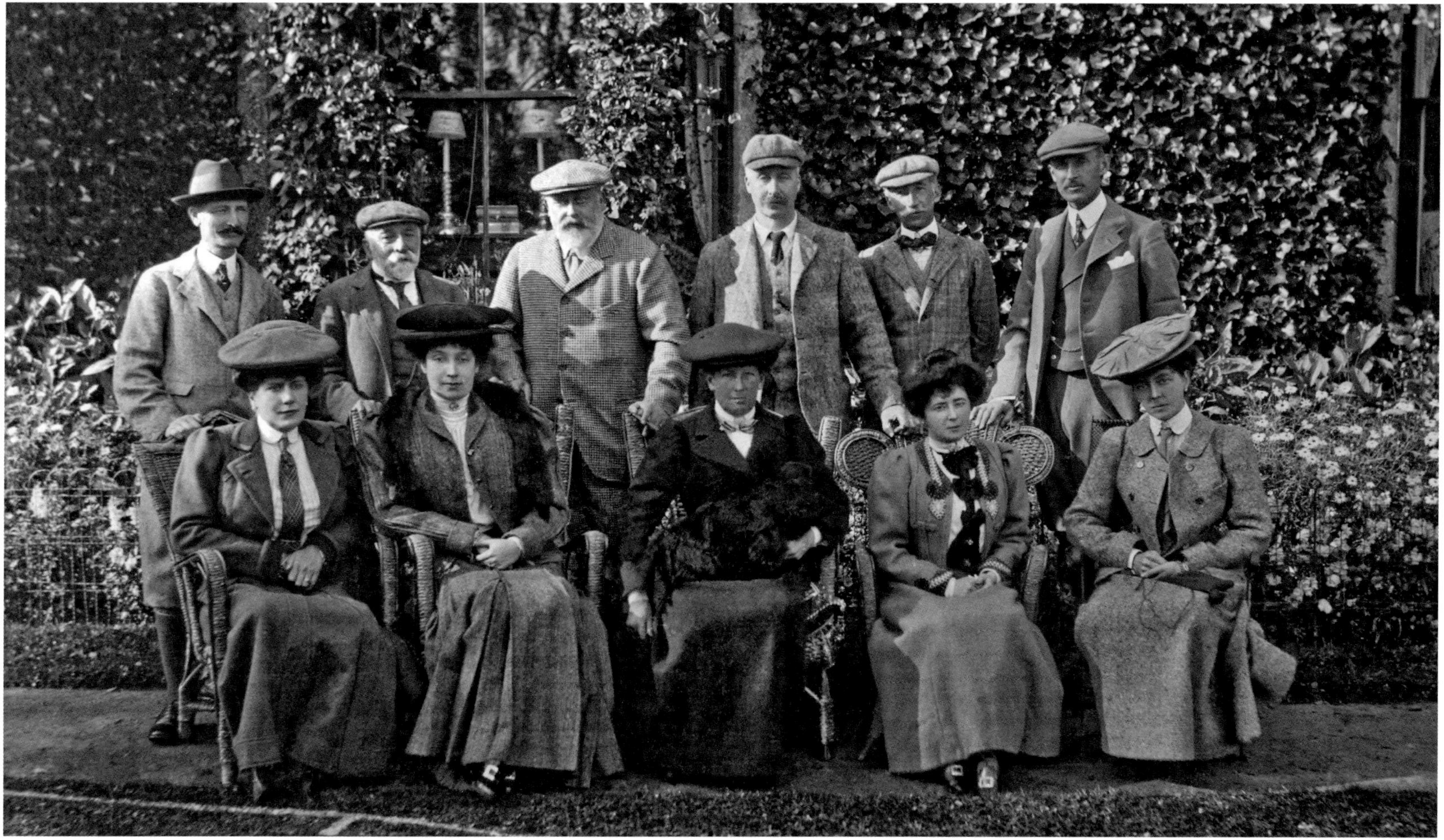

Tulchan Lodge near Advie, on the Seafield estate, was favoured by 'new money' in the nineteenth century; Michael T. Bass, the brewery magnate, first leased the grouse shootings in 1849. In the 1880s Arthur D. Sassoon became the lessee. The Sassoon brothers were members of the 'Marlborough House Set' of the Prince of Wales (later King Edward VII), and many royals, including King George V and later his son, the Duke of Gloucester, visited Tulchan; the Great North of Scotland's Advie Station even had a 'Royal Waiting Room'. A new lodge at Dalchroy, two miles away, was built in 1906 and is now known as 'Tulchan' while the original is now named Knocktulchan and used for smaller groups. In this house party of 1906, photographed at the original Tulchan Lodge, King Edward VII is in the back row, third left, while his friend Alice, Mrs George Keppel, is on the far left of the front row.

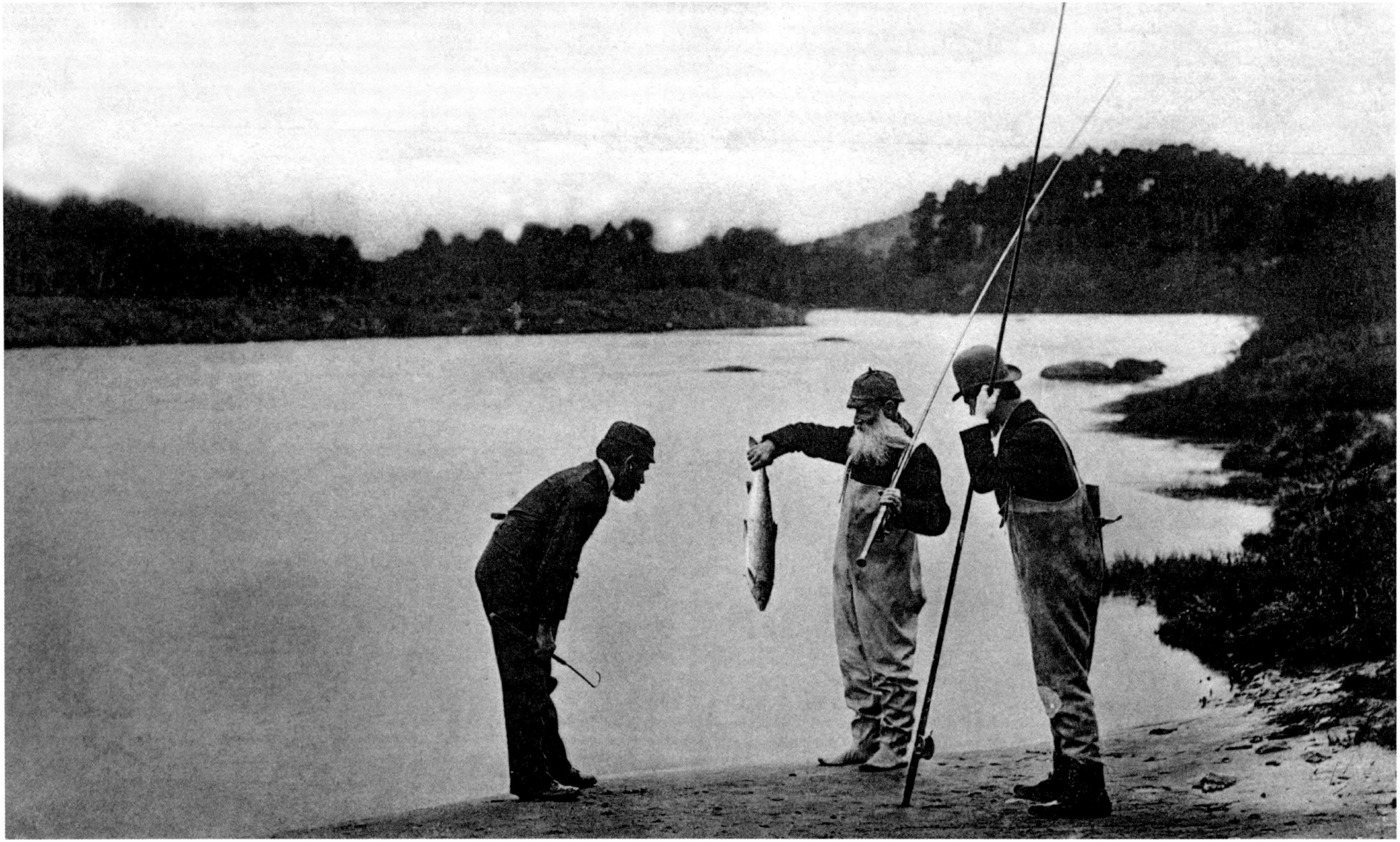

The River Spey is one of the finest salmon rivers in Scotland. Hazards up to the 1890s were 'vast floats of timber' in rafts going to the Moray coast at Garmouth. Manmade 'cruives' of stones to trap fish and the netting of migrating salmon at the river mouth were problems preventing their passage upstream, and bailiffs also had to check poaching. This photograph shows anglers in the late nineteenth century with a ghillie in attendance. By the 1930s the Strathspey Angling Association was leasing thirteen miles of riversides and offering season tickets at 'extremely moderate charges' (according to a Strathspey Angling Association advertisement of 1934). The average number of salmon taken each year was 150, while sea trout were very numerous.

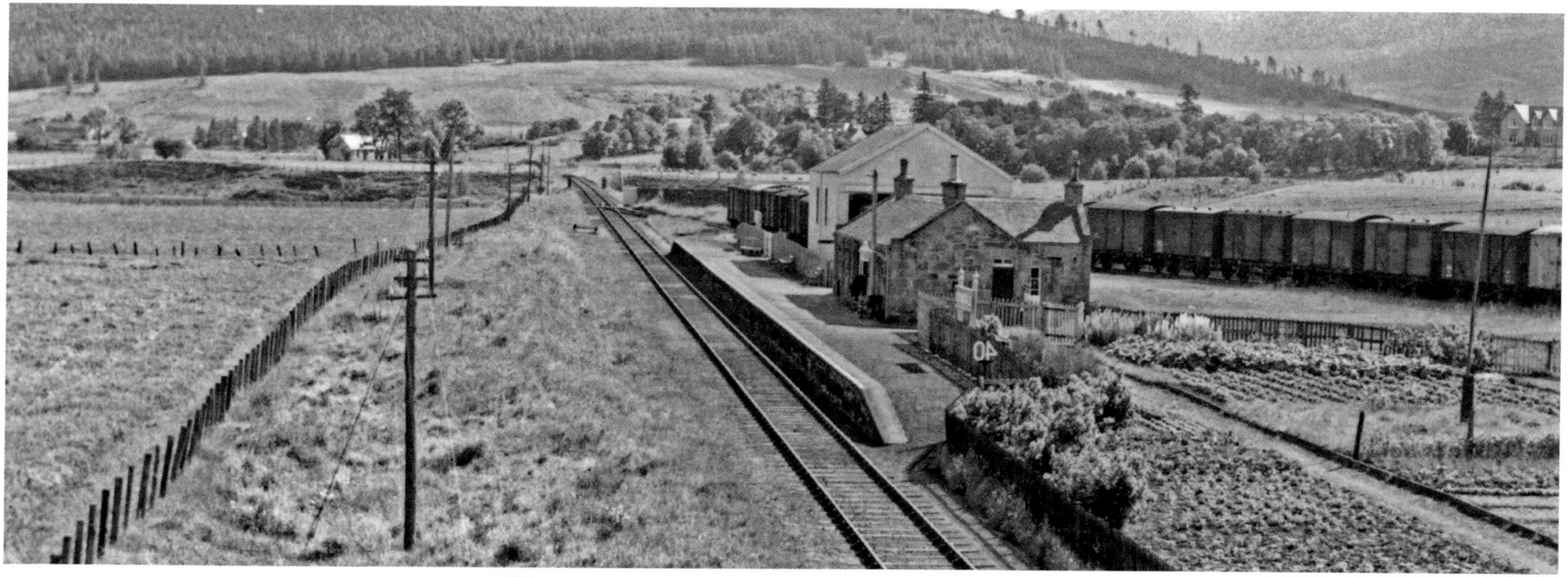

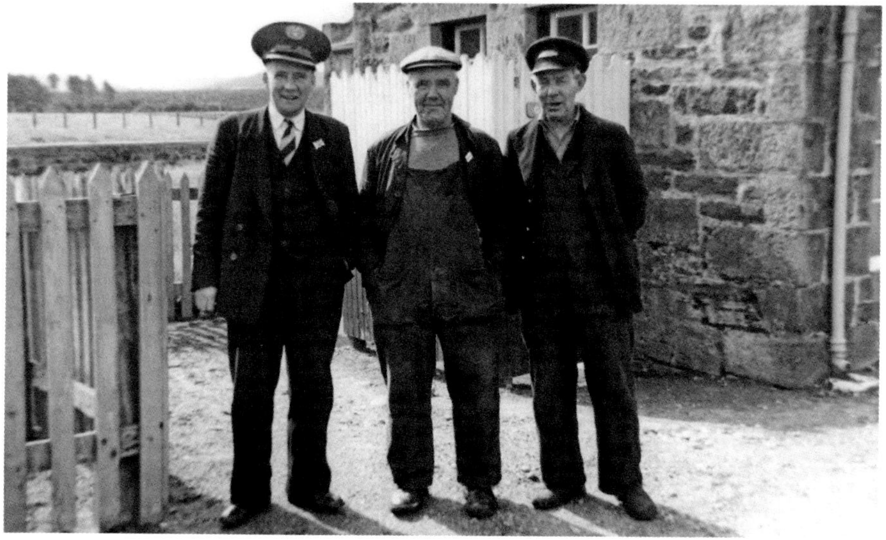

Cromdale Station dated from 1865 when the Strathspey Railway, later part of the Great North of Scotland Railway, was progressing southwards along the valley. The station was granite built and had a timber goods shed and an ample siding, here holding freight vans. Cromdale also had a branch line to Balmenach Distillery, served by its own small locomotive, 'Balmenach', now preserved at Boat of Garten on the Strathspey Railway. Typically, the station had a flourishing garden (right), which was tended by staff. The staff shown here are the last stationmaster, William Smith, Billy Ross the surfaceman, and the porter, Jock McPherson. The station was closed in 1965 but this section is now part of the Speyside Way walking route and the station has been handsomely restored.

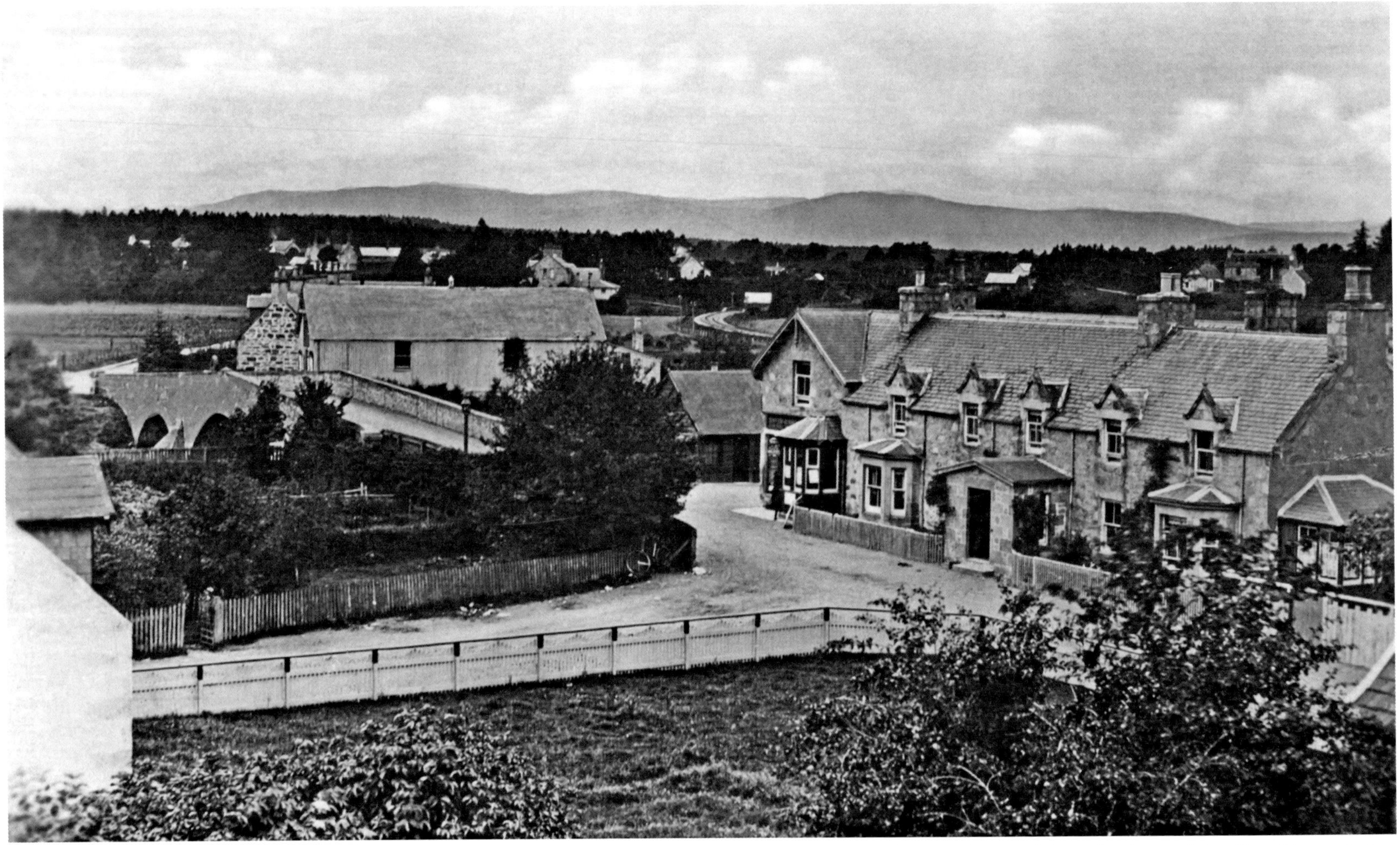

In the late eighteenth century, using various means (mostly through tenants providing 'statute labour'), James Grant of Grant had over 130 miles of 'remarkably good' road made including 'an excellent bridge', a two-arch structure over the River Nethy, which attracted a settlement around it. Unfortunately, a flood in 1799 destroyed this so the Commission for Highland Roads and Bridges, with Thomas Telford as their engineer, contributed half the cost of new bridges in Abernethy around 1810 (the village would not take its current name until later in the nineteenth century). Across the river, just beyond the replacement bridge, the drill hall for the local Territorials, the 3rd Battalion Seaforth Highlanders, can be seen. This building was removed in the 1960s.

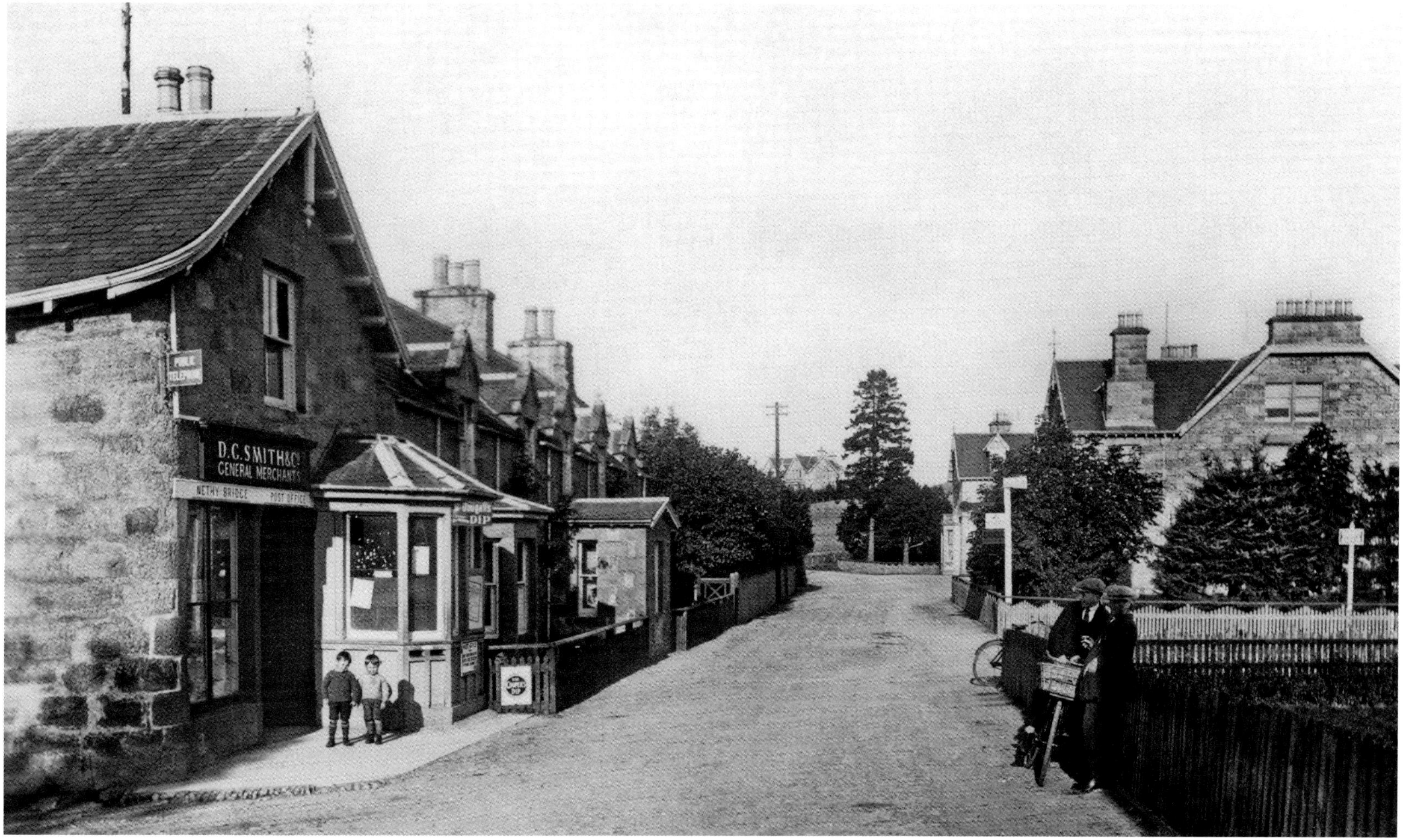


Where the Grantown road approached the bridge over the River Nethy, this post office building replaced old premises at Duack Bridge in the 1870s, giving better access to and from the railway and the nearby hotel. In the 1920s D.G. Smith combined the post office with a general merchants' business. Smith's had a public telephone and stocked a range of goods both for visitors – it sold its own postcards – and for the farming community, such as McDougall's Sheep Dip. The shop was strategically placed where roads met and it is now a bunkhouse close to the Speyside Way. The Nethybridge Hotel is on the right of the photograph.

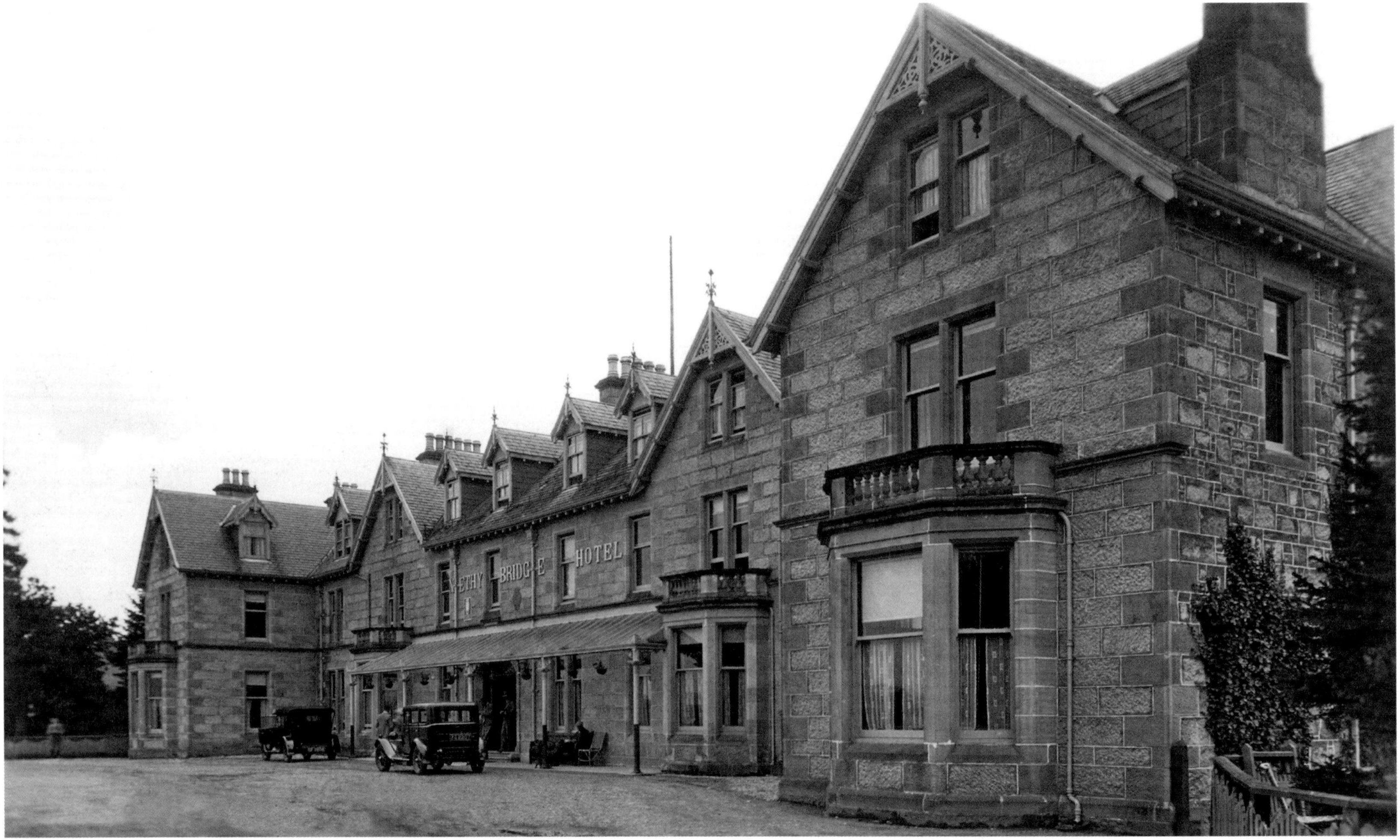


Nethybridge Hotel dates from the early 1880s when James Forbes Grant took the premises on a 99-year lease. Increasing number of visitors were coming thanks to the railways; by 1865 the village was served by two companies, the Highland Railway and the Great North of Scotland Railway, resulting in the old name of Abernethy being changed to Nethybridge to prevent confusion with Abernethy in Perthshire. In 1893 a bridge was constructed across the River Spey at Broomhill, also improving access to the village. With its large garden and farm at Coulnakyle supplying fresh produce for guests, the hotel was so successful that it was enlarged in 1912.

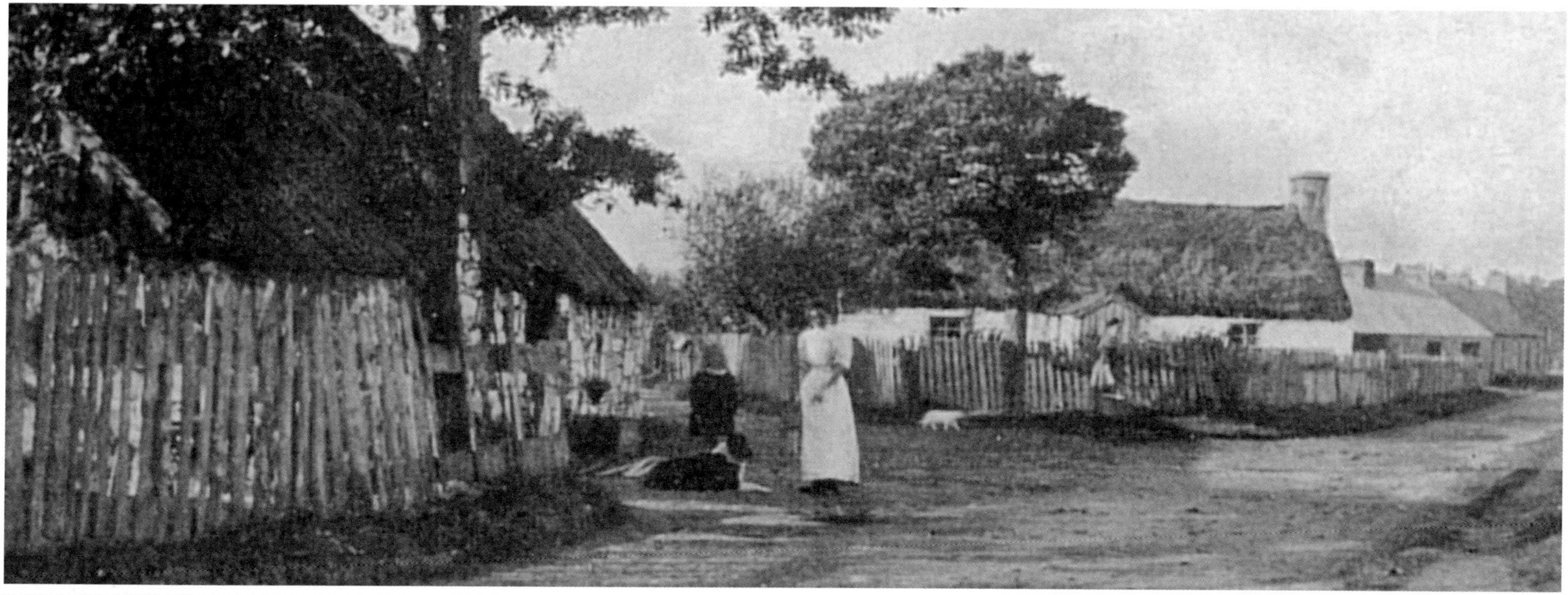

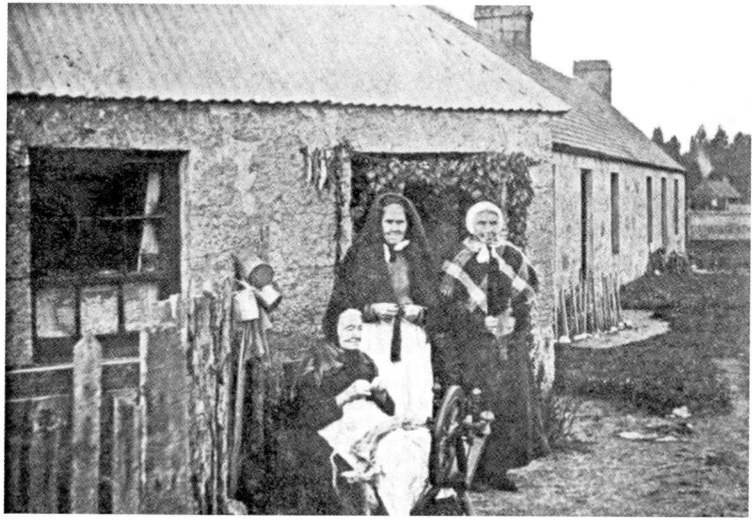

Causer, at Nethybridge, is probably from the Gaelic 'cabhsair' meaning a paved road, possibly from the iron-smelting years of the 1730s. In 1870, it consisted of six cottages, a poor's houses and a smithy. The latter (on the left) was built in 1806 at a crossroads and was roofed with 'backs', the outer trimmings of logs. A blacksmith occupied the smithy until 1971 but it is now holiday accommodation. The Causer has grown with both council and private housing beside the primary school for Nethybridge.

This photograph appeared on a Christmas card of 1903, which was unusual as Scots chose to ignore Christmas but instead marked Hogmanay and New Year's Day. It shows three octogenarian women knitting and spinning outside a cottage at Causer. They are wearing 'mutches', a traditional head covering, and have shawls to keep warm. The cottages, dating from the 1860s, are stone built with galvanised iron or slate roofs. Note the milk cans on the fence and fish drying by the door.

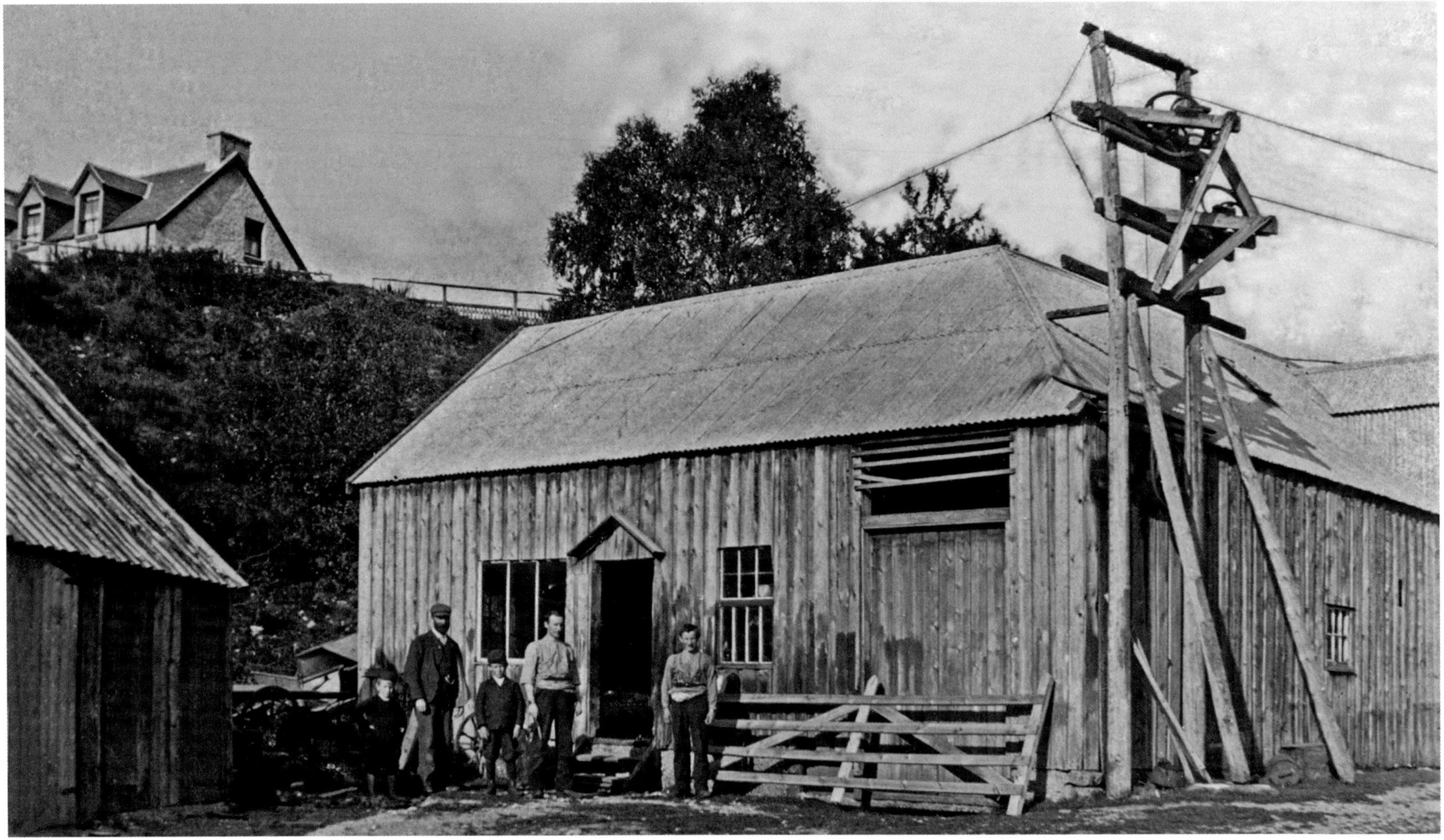

Balnagowan (which translates as the 'homestead of the smith') at Nethybridge was once the site of iron smelting. After the 1715 Jacobite rising, the York Buildings Company, an English concern, purchased the forfeited estates of Jacobite sympathisers, thus becoming the biggest landowner in Scotland. At that time scarcity of charcoal was forcing iron companies to use Highland resources of Scots pine. Iron ore was mined at the Lecht until 1737 and carried in panniers by ponies to this site where waterpower from the Nethy was an attraction. From the 1870s Balnagowan was a sawmill leased to the Macdonalds and by the 1900s the then lessee Alexander McPherson used an aerial cableway for transporting timber across the Nethy valley to the sawmill. These cableways were commonly used in extractive industries such as coal mines and clay pits and were also referred to as 'Blondins' after the tightrope expert.

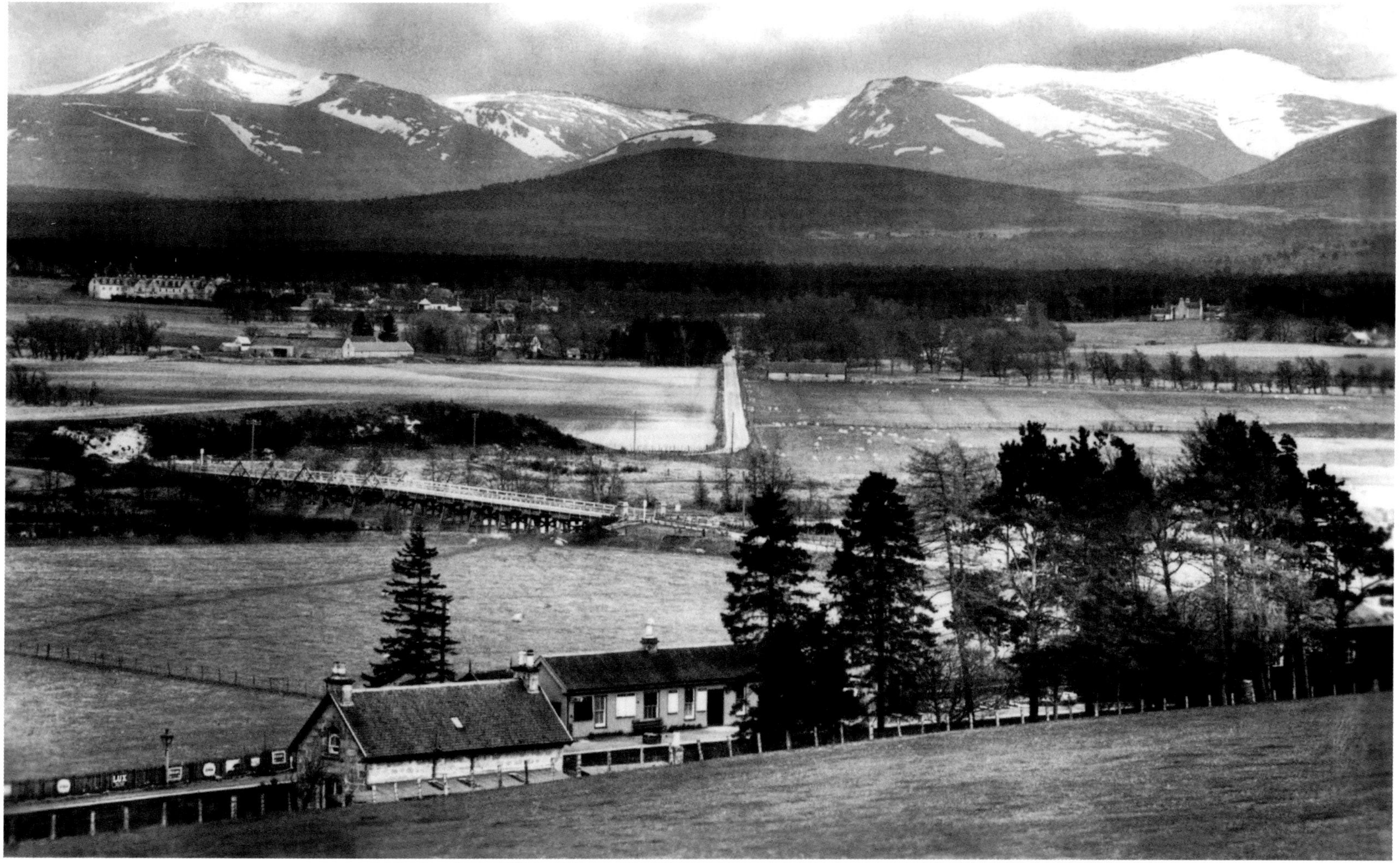

This view extends from snow-covered Bynack Mor at 3,574 feet (left) to Cairn Gorm at 4,084 feet (right). Broomhill Station in the foreground was on the main line through the Grampians via Forres to Inverness, which opened in 1863. Two years later it became part of the Highland Railway. The timber bridge over the River Spey replaced a ferry at the Boat of Broomhill and was built in 1893. The road leads to Nethybridge. The station is now served by the Strathspey Railway's heritage steam-hauled trains and achieved fame as 'Glenbogle' in the TV series *Monarch of the Glen*.

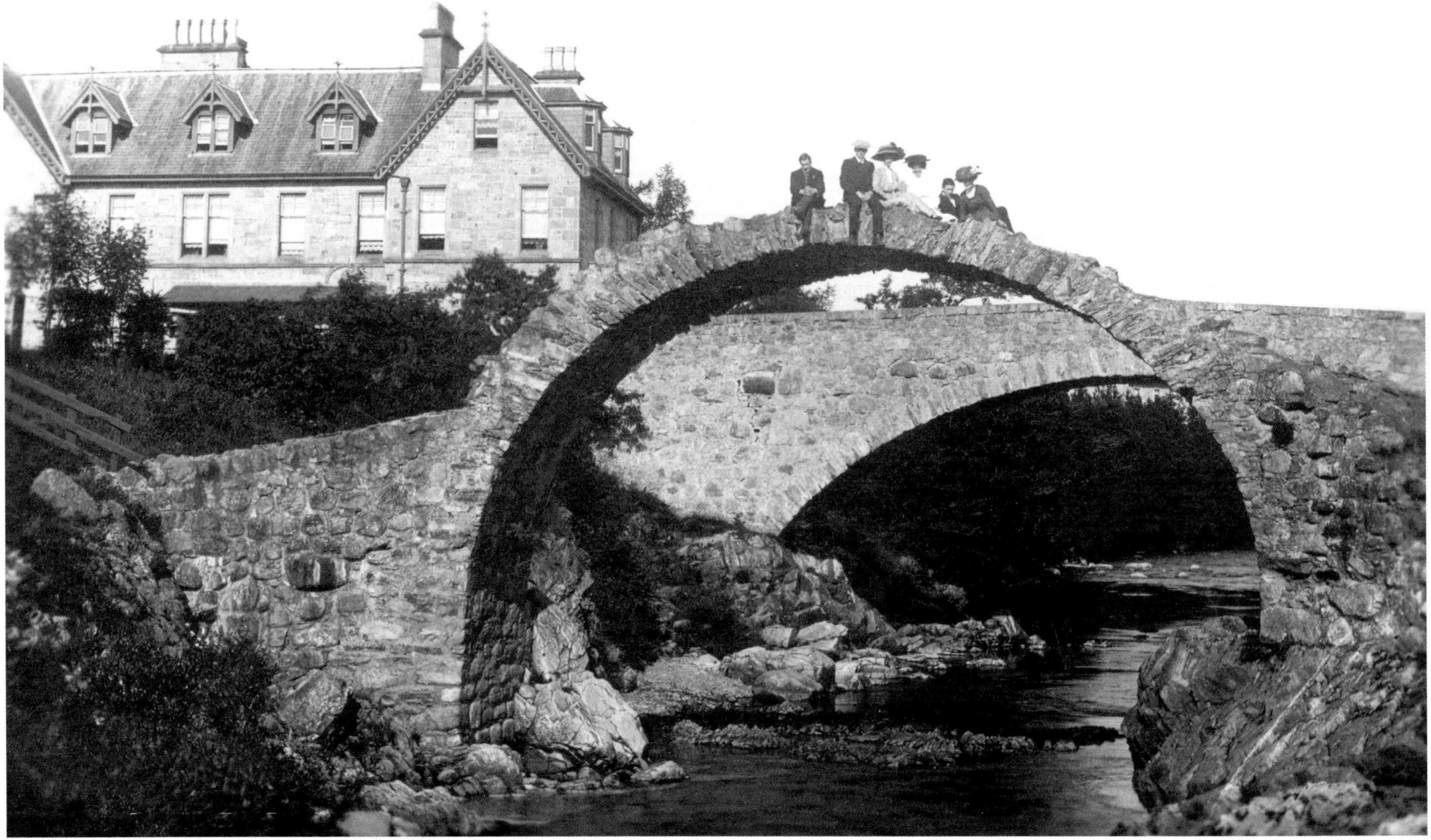

The old bridge across the River Dulnain at Carrbridge was built in 1717 for parishioners accessing Duthil Parish Church on the north bank of the river. Constructed at the Linn of Dalrachney, where rock outcropped, it is the oldest surviving bridge in the Highlands. Widened in 1760 to accommodate carriages, it became a focal point and by 1790 there was an inn beside it, an initiative by the laird, now Sir James Grant of Grant. This was later replaced by a hotel (left), which was enlarged in 1892 and again in 1911. In the background is the Telford bridge of 1818, erected by the Commission for Highland Roads and Bridges.

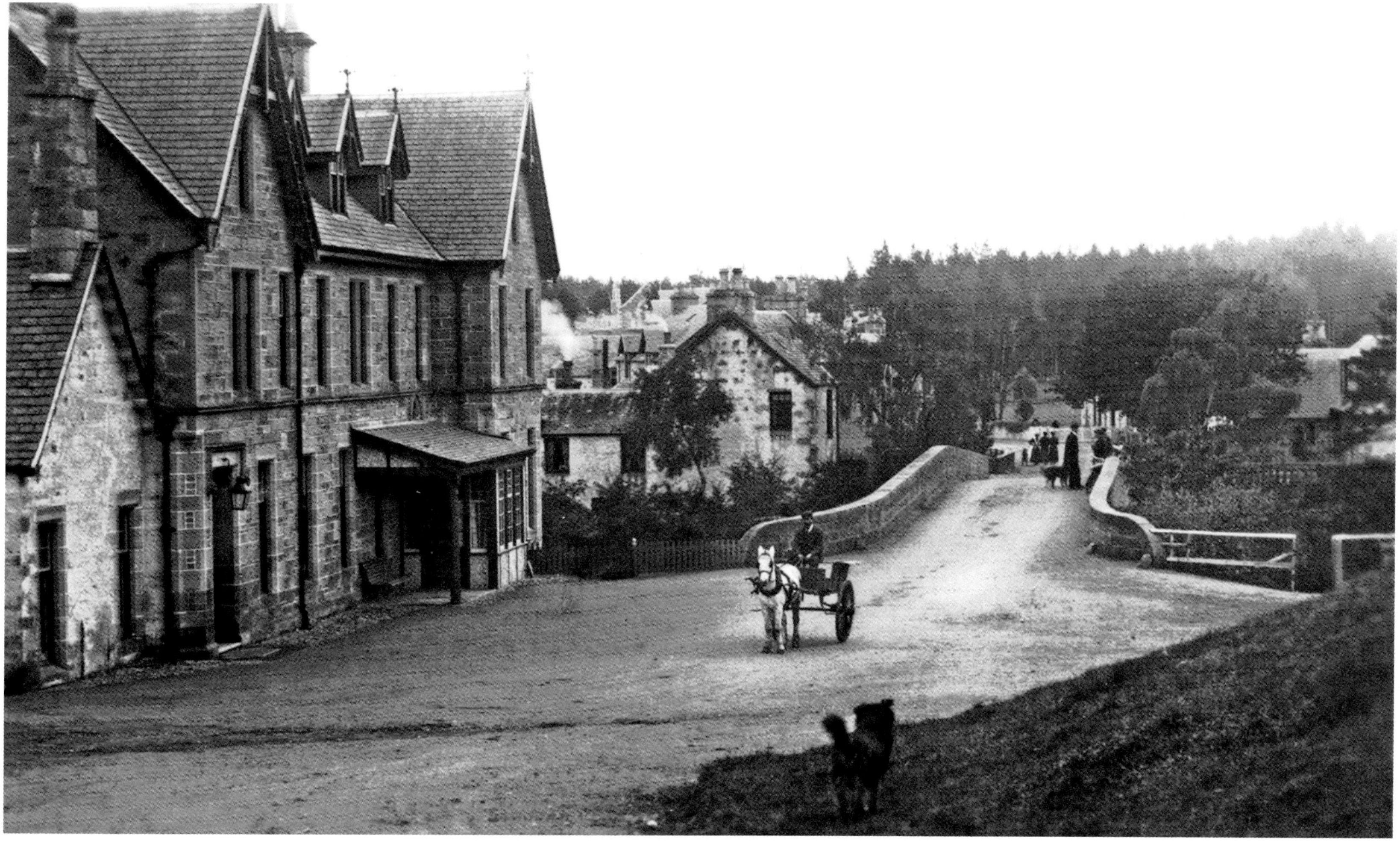

In *Slater's Directory* for 1860, the Carrbridge Hotel (left) is noted as a 'family, commercial and posting house' (where coach horses were changed). After the Highland Railway opened to Carrbridge in 1892, visitor numbers grew and the hotel's capacity was increased. Nearby a smithy is belching smoke. Many men were employed in estate forestry and the hotel's public bar was popular. This view looks south over the narrow Telford bridge of 1818 which was replaced with a reinforced concrete structure in the latter 1920s. The Duthil road (now the A938), with military associations from the 1750s, branches left, while on the right is the Telford route to Inverness, later followed by the old A9.

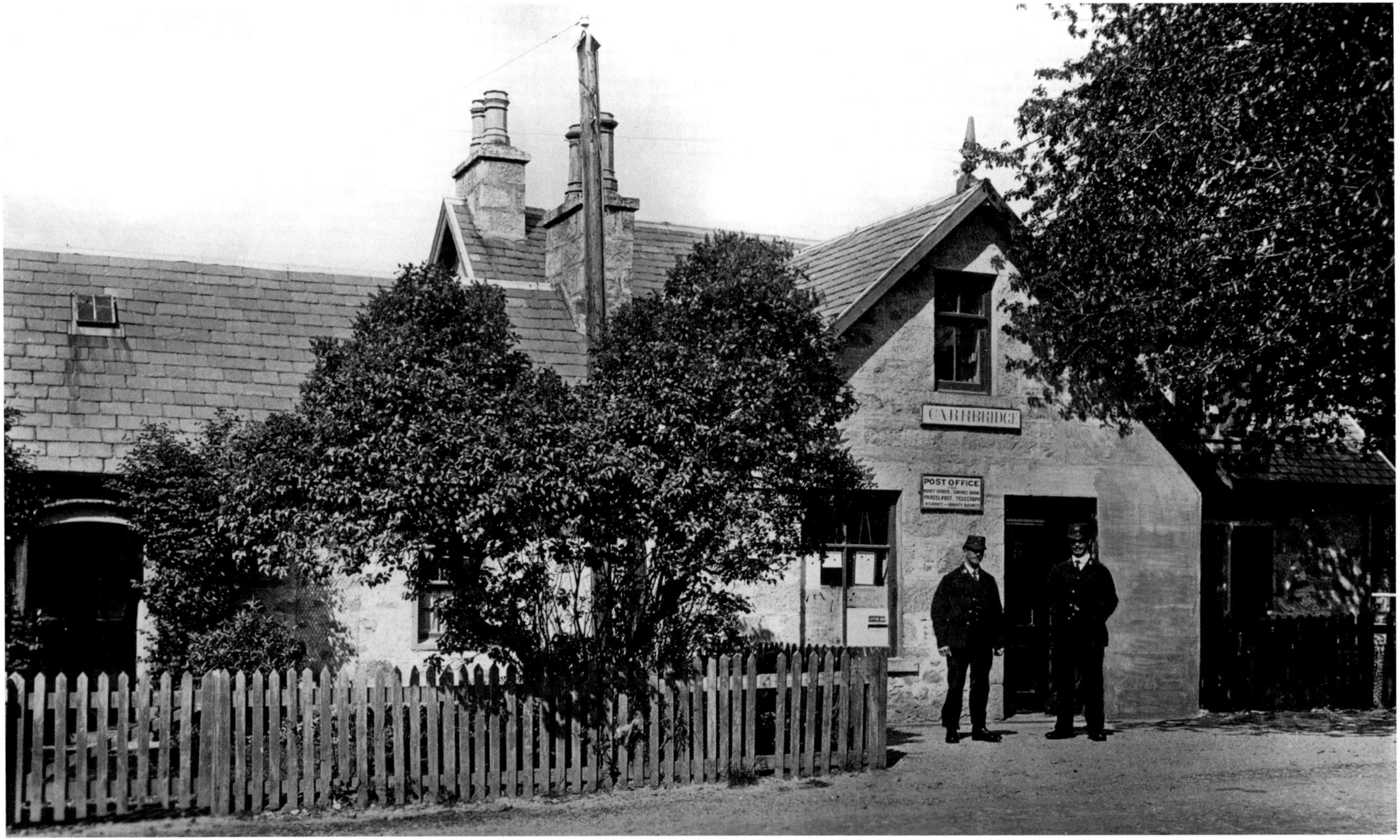


Until the nineteenth century the Highlands' delivery of mail was uncertain – the Carrbridge area had only an irregular service. Even after 1818, when Telford had improved the routes for the Commission for Highland Roads and Bridges, the Post Office still refused a direct service, the mails from the south coming via Aberdeen. The defile of Slochd Mhuic was an obstacle only made safe after 1835 for Royal Mail coaches which ran between Perth and Inverness via Carrbridge. From 1863 the railway won the Royal Mail contract and by 1892, when the Highland Railway's Carrbridge Branch from Aviemore opened, a post office offering telegraph and financial services had been combined with a village shop, which continues in use.

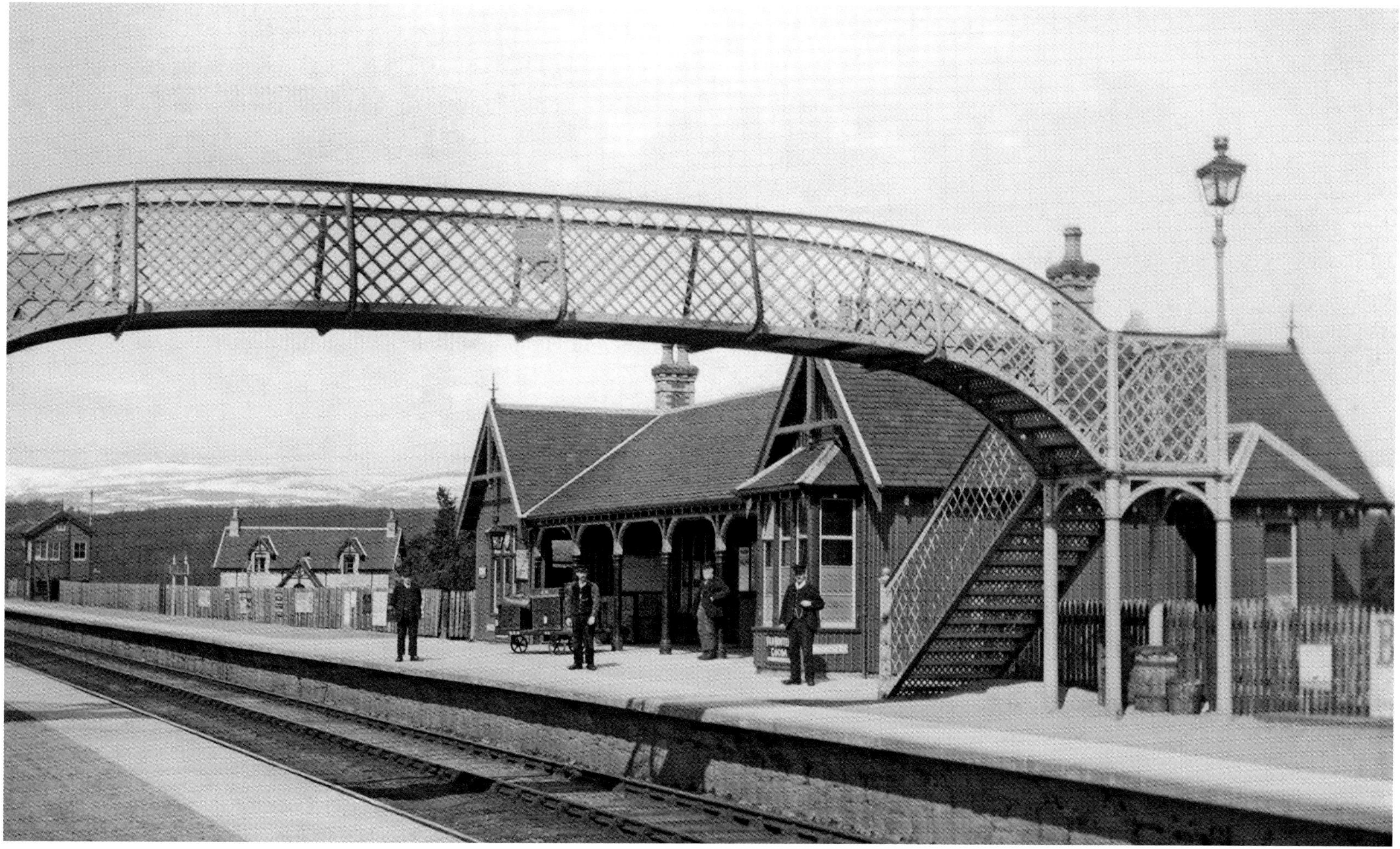

Carrbridge Station was opened as a temporary terminus in 1892 to serve branch trains from Aviemore, which thereby became a junction. The signal box (far left) and station with its sheltering veranda were of timber construction but the stationmaster's house (left of centre) was stone built. The staff, with conspicuous watch chains, made sure the trains ran to time – a challenge on the largely single-track HR system. The expensive direct line to Inverness via Carrbridge resulted from railway politics as it prevented an attempt by the Great North of Scotland Railway to access Inverness and steal HR business there.

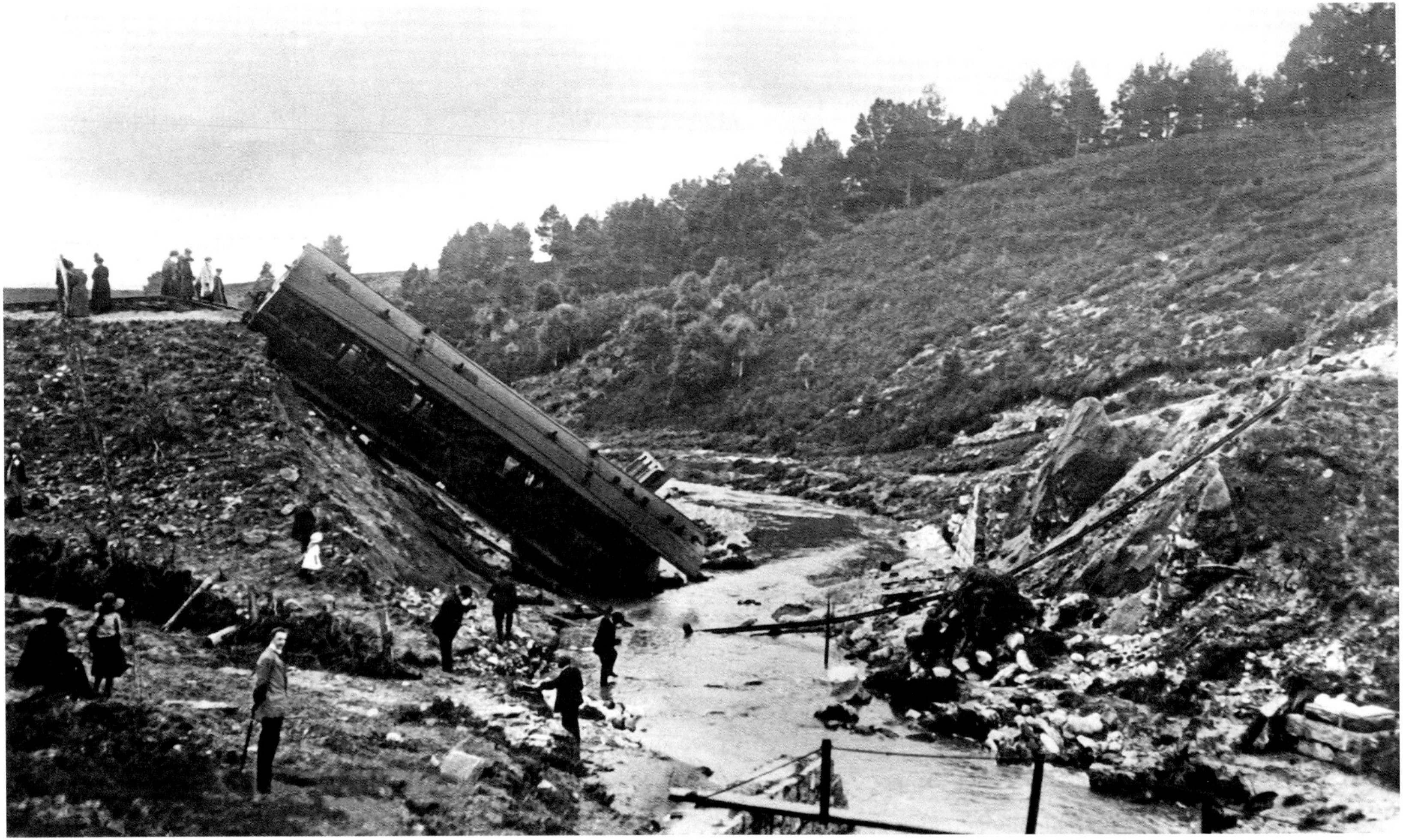

On 18 June 1914 violent thunderstorms assailed the Highlands and the Baddengorm Burn, fed from bare hills west of Carrbridge, became a raging torrent. When the 11.50 a.m. train from Perth, due at Carrbridge in the afternoon, reached the bridge over the burn, the arch was jammed with tree trunks and debris ponding back 20 feet of water. The locomotive got across but the track gave way, throwing carriages into the flood. Five passengers were lost and nine injured. Working round the clock, the contractors McAlpine's had the line reopened in three weeks. In July 1923 there was another flash flood in the area; no train was involved, although the scale of damage to the line was even more extensive.

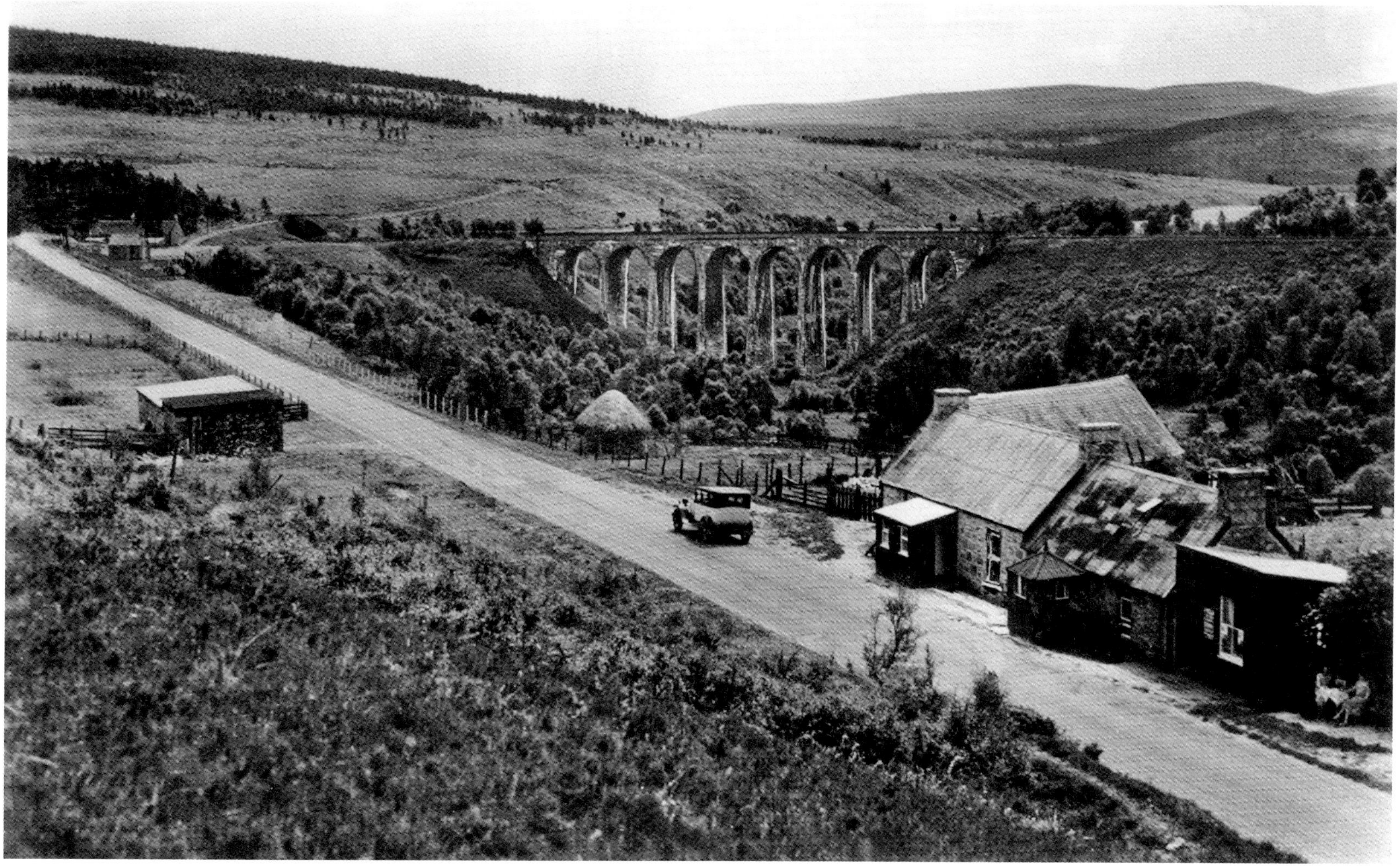

This alignment of the Great North Road at Slochd Mhuic dates from 1928 when a motor road was constructed close to the Telford route of 1835. The cottage was once a tollhouse – the booth is intact – with tollgates at which travellers had to pay up. Note the initiative of a tea table to serve motorists. In the background is the Slochd viaduct on the direct line to Inverness. This route was known as the 'Aviemore Deviation' and cost the Highland Railway dear as three major viaducts were required on it. Opened in 1898, it is the line followed today from the south to Inverness.

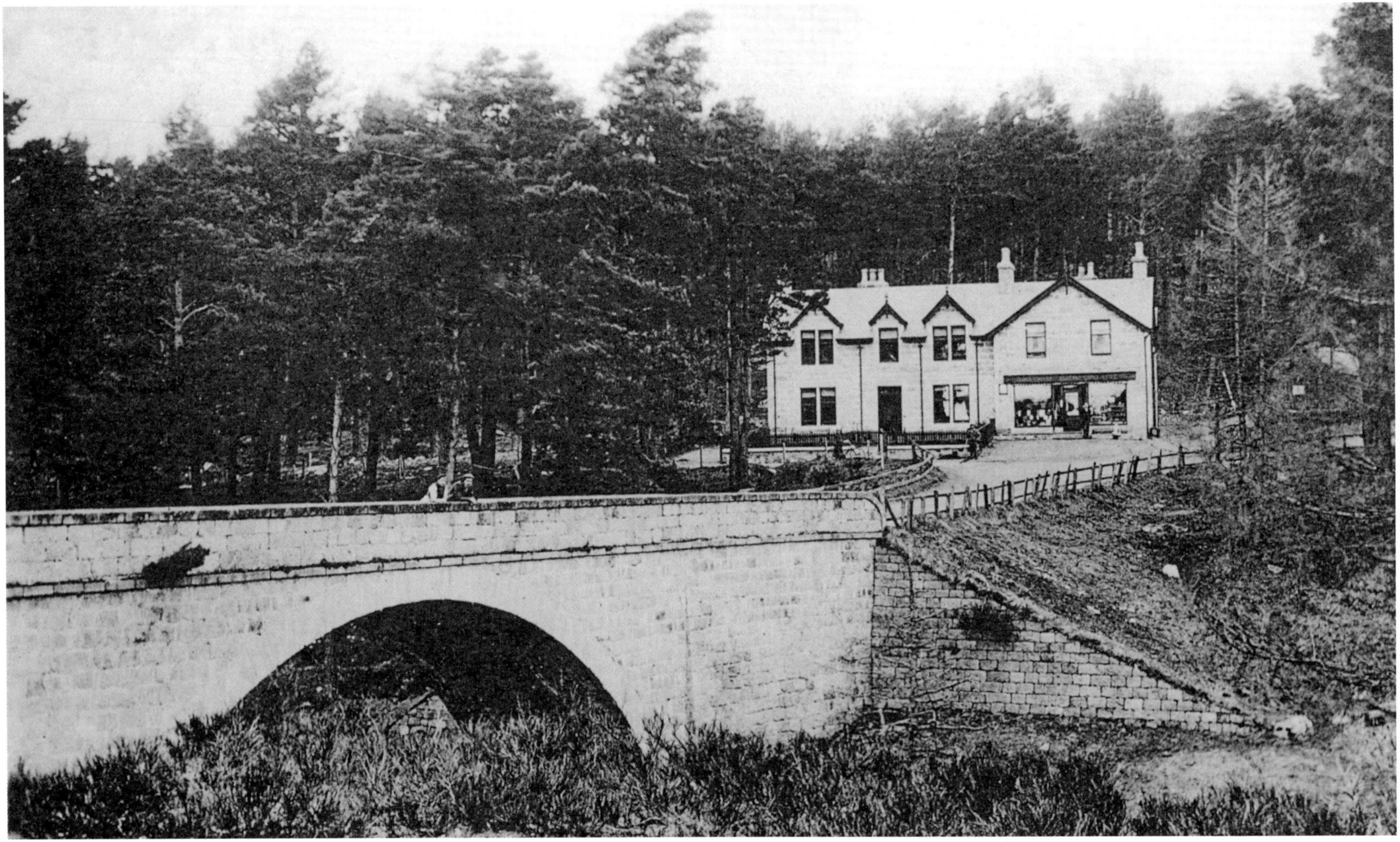

Dulnain Bridge lies on the river of that name (properly termed 'Dulnan'), a tributary of the Spey. A bridge was constructed here in 1754 on a military road from Aviemore to Castle Grant and was rebuilt in 1791. Damaged in the Moray Floods of 1829, it was repaired by the Commission for Highland Roads and Bridges. Close by is the former crofting township of Skye of Curr. There, tradesmen settled, growing crops and rearing cattle and sheep. Now some 40 houses – new builds or reconstructions – occupy the old croftland. The former Calders' village store and post office, placed at the crossroads, still supplies provisions to the community.

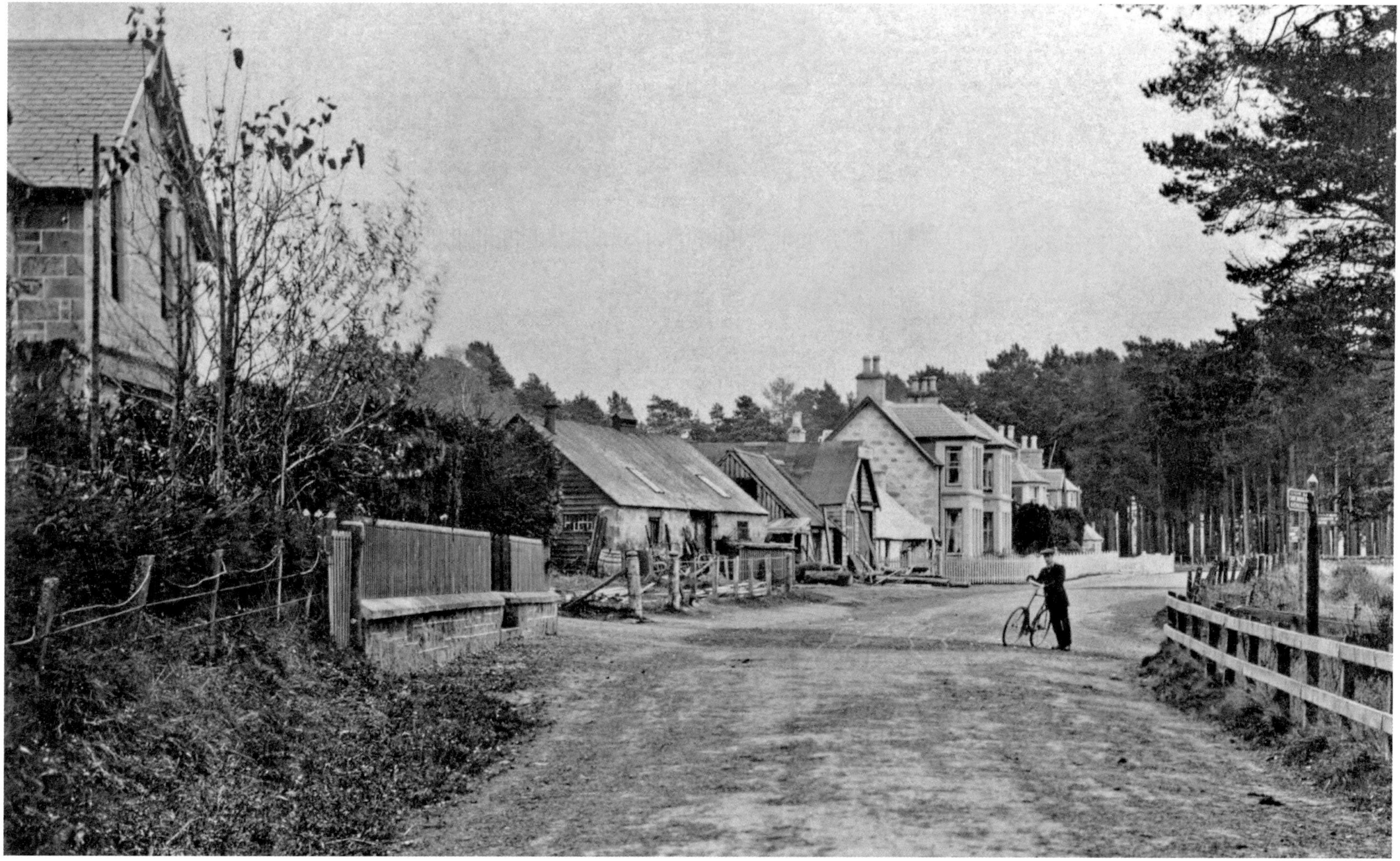

Looking east from the bridge end at Dulnain Bridge along the road to Grantown in the 1900s, this photograph shows the village store combined with the post office on the left, and next to it, the old smithy where James McDonald plied his trade for many years. In the 1930s, the smithy was replaced by petrol pumps and motor repair facilities. Further along the road newly built letting properties for summer visitors are seen. The wooden signposts, at the crossroads of the Dulnainside route with the road from Aviemore, assisted cyclists and walkers, and increasingly motorists, in exploring the district.

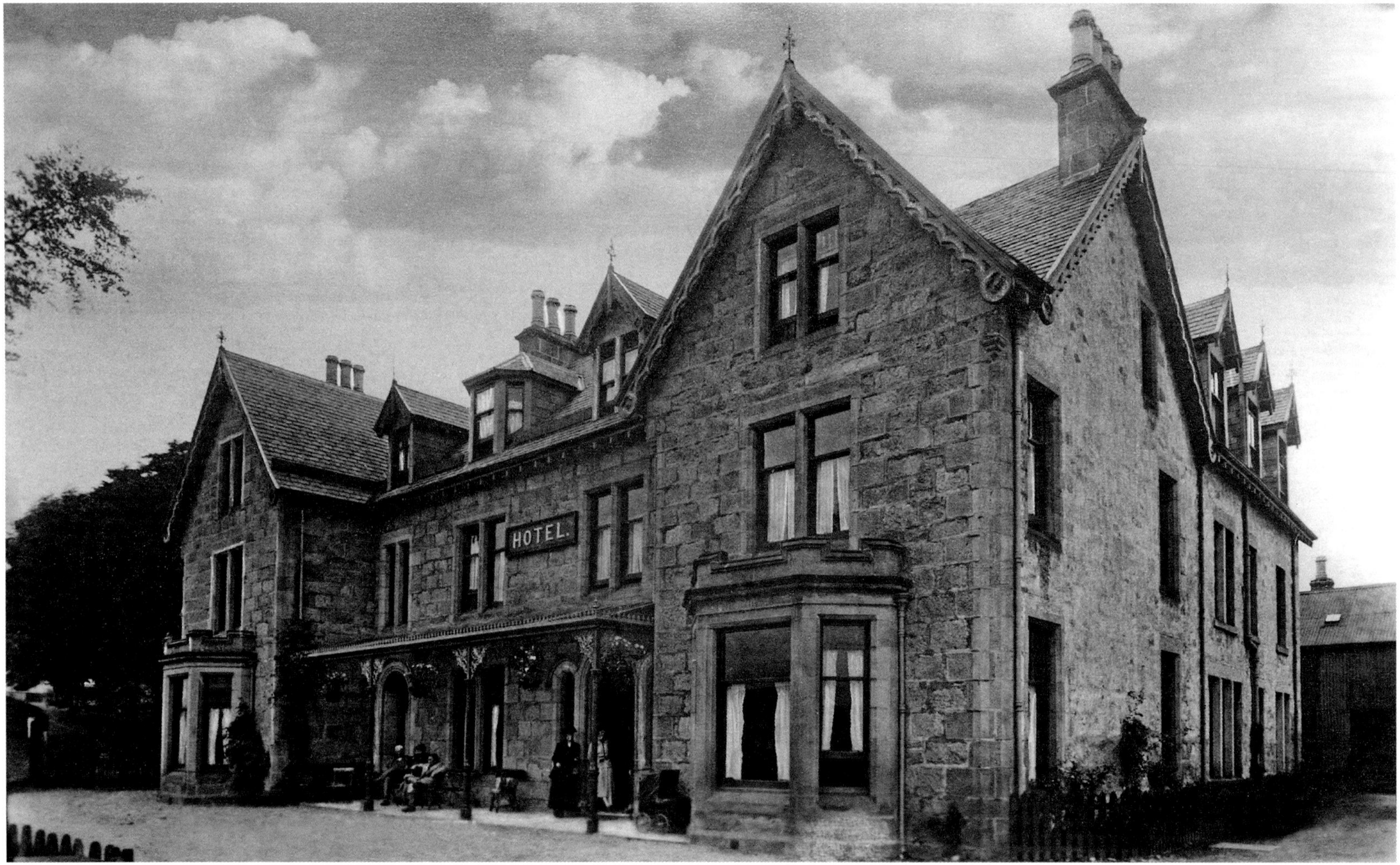


Boat of Garten Hotel was built on the site of Macgregor's inn, which served as a 'howff' for navvies constructing the Inverness & Perth Junction Railway in the early 1860s. The site was transformed in the 1880s by the building of this hotel, run by George Grant; conveniently, it faced the railway station, which was a junction from 1866. Shown here in 1925, the hotel attracted not only holidaymakers looking for accommodation but also locals as it had a public bar, a separate galvanised-iron structure seen on the right. Down the years, fires led to the hotel being reconstructed and the entrance now faces the main road.

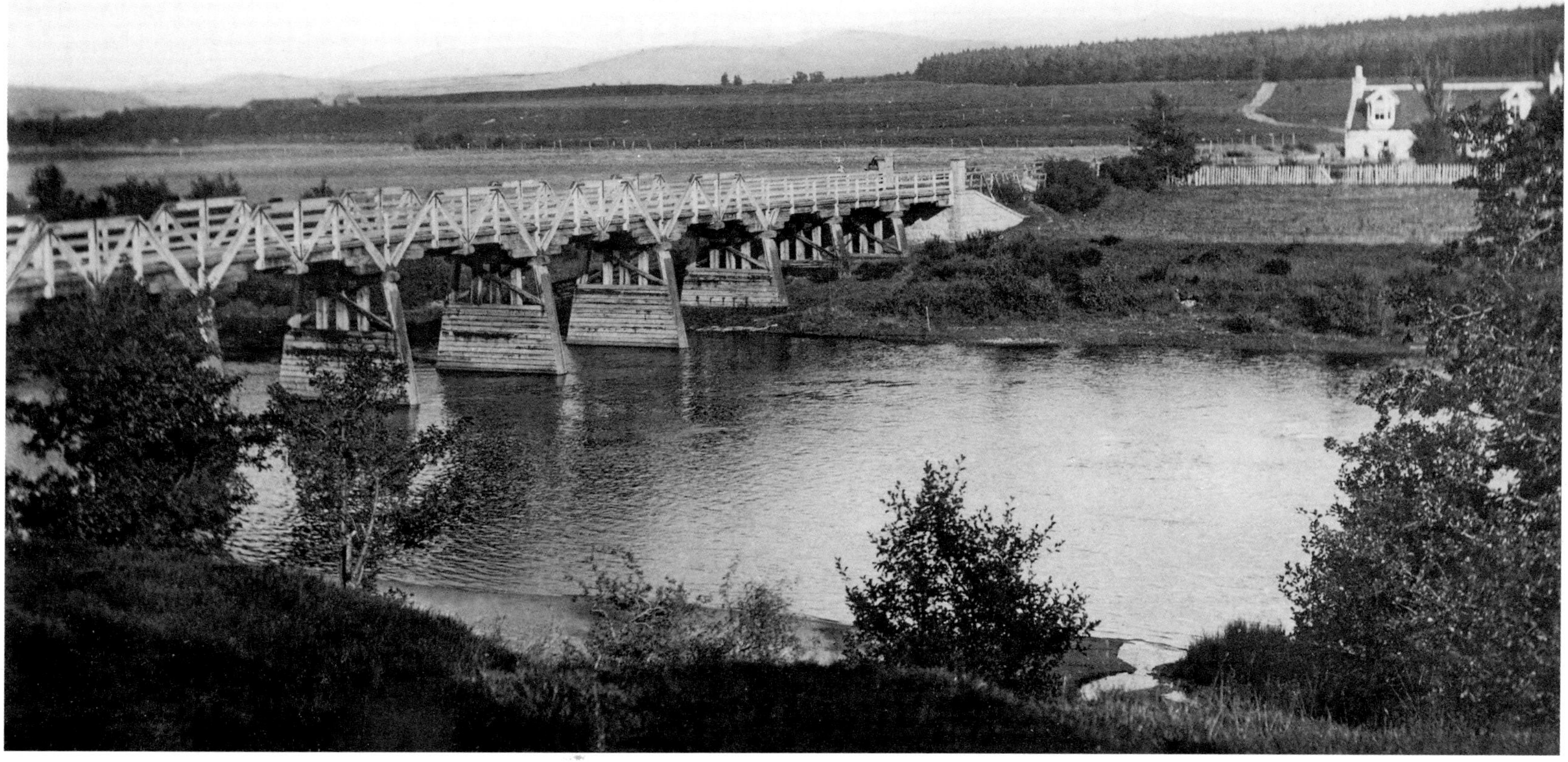

An old ford on the River Spey was in time replaced by a ferry at what became Boat of Garten. A chain operated 'pontoon' capable of taking vehicles was in action by the 1880s and the house of James Cameron (Jimmie Boatie), the last ferryman, can be seen on the right. This timber bridge, designed by Alexander Mackenzie, a Kingussie architect and engineer, was built in 1899. During the Second World War when attempts were made by Royal Engineers to strengthen the structure, it was set on fire by a blowlamp and a ferry had to be improvised while the bridge was repaired. A new bridge was constructed here in 1974.

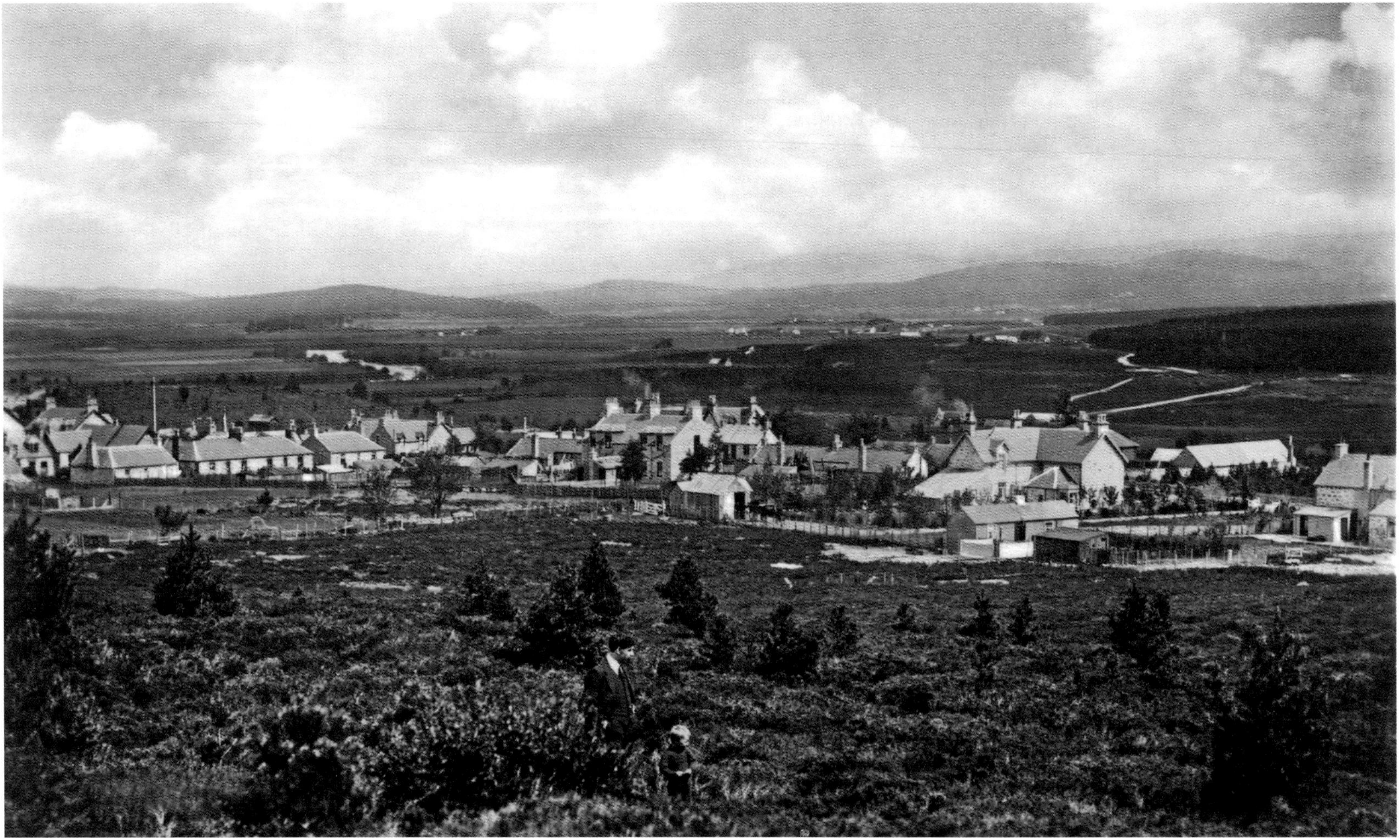

Looking north over Boat of Garten in the early 1900s reveals how much the place had grown since the coming of the railway in 1863. The main street, now Deshar Road (on the left), has Highland Railway cottages for staff and, behind these, a tall flagpole marks the public hall. In the centre of the view are more railway houses, the hotel and the station. On the right are large villas which were let to summer visitors while their owners meanwhile made do with simple accommodation, often of galvanised iron, in the back gardens. Beyond, the strath's haughlands are speckled with farms. This view is now lost through the growth of tree cover in the foreground area.

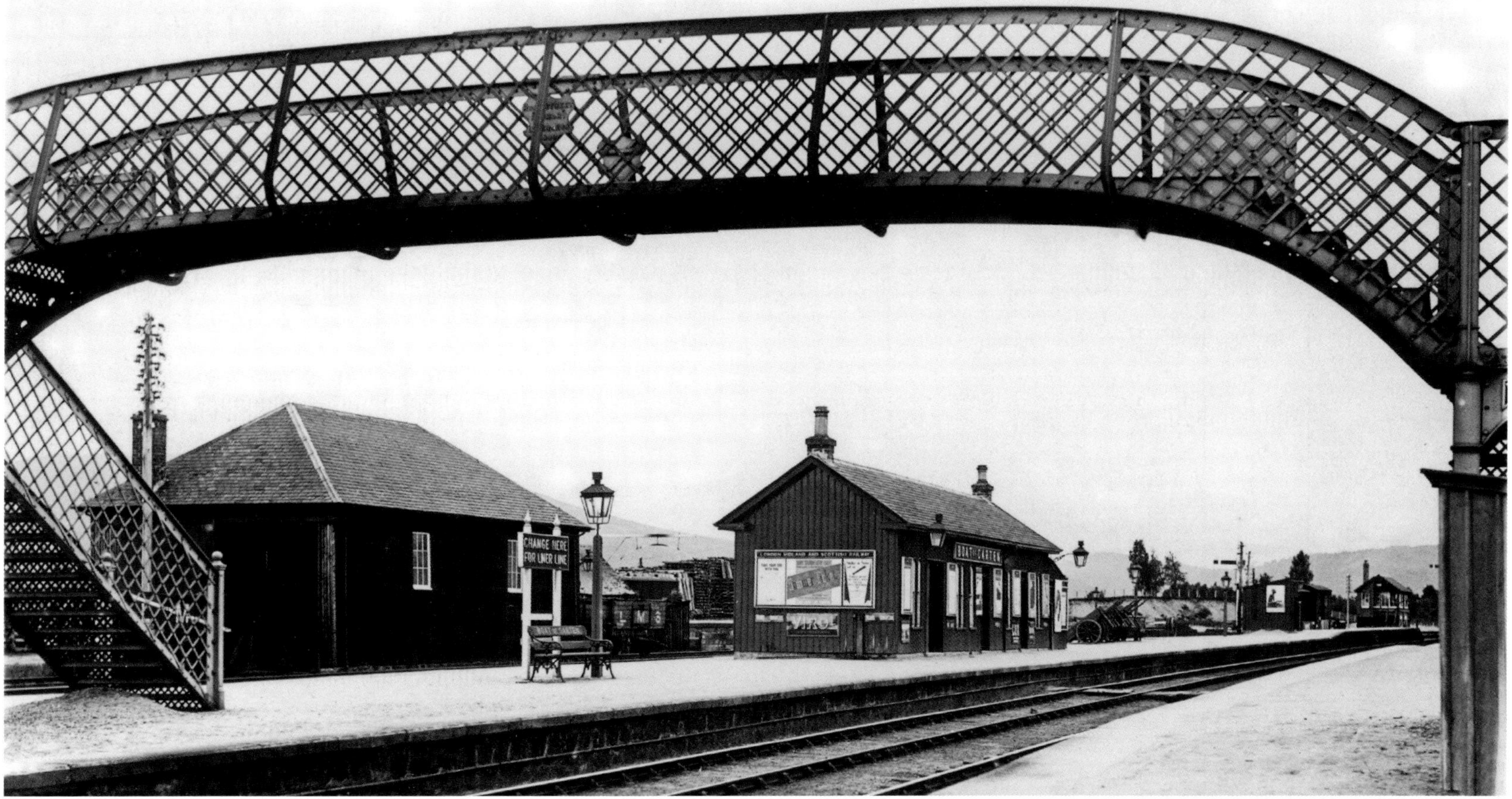


Boat of Garten Station was opened by the Inverness & Perth Junction Railway in 1863, becoming a junction when the Strathspey Railway, under the Great North of Scotland Railway, advanced from Abernethy (now Nethybridge) three years later. Disagreements led to a separate track being laid for the GNSR from near Broomhill to 'The Boat'. By 1865, the I&PJR had become part of the Highland Railway, which controlled this station for almost sixty years. This view is from the interwar period when the London, Midland & Scottish and the London & North Eastern Railway companies were in existence. The heritage Strathspey Railway reopened the line from Aviemore in 1978 and the footbridge from the Rose Street Foundry in Inverness was moved further south.

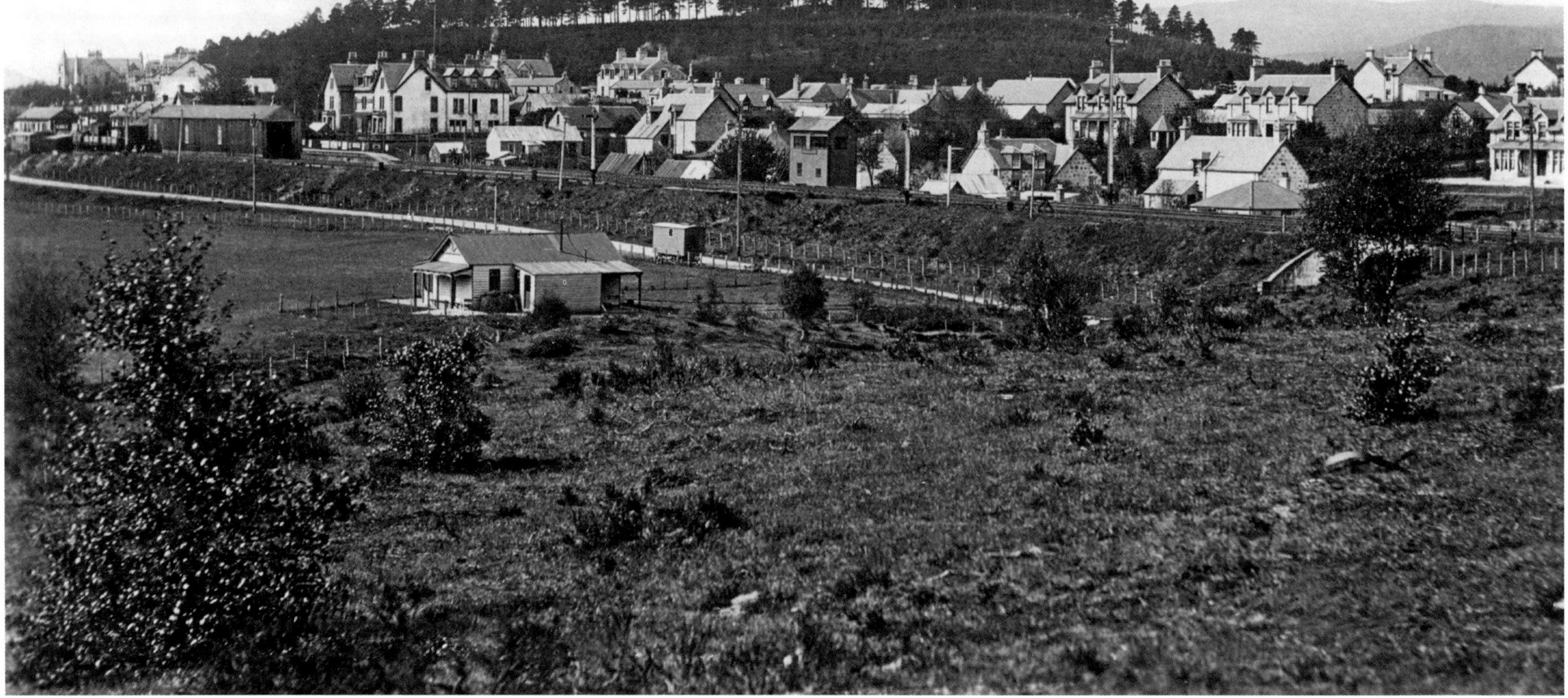

Boat of Garten, viewed from the north around 1910; the then new golf clubhouse is in the foreground and the junction station with its embankment and installations is just above it. Here the Great North of Scotland Railway met the Highland Railway in 1866. Unofficial races took place on the parallel tracks between the rivals' trains from south of Broomhill into 'The Boat', as Boat of Garten is known locally. The hotel and the villas, let by the month to summer visitors, are clearly visible while the hill known as Craig Garten or 'the Craigie', a fine vantage point, has only a fringe of trees.

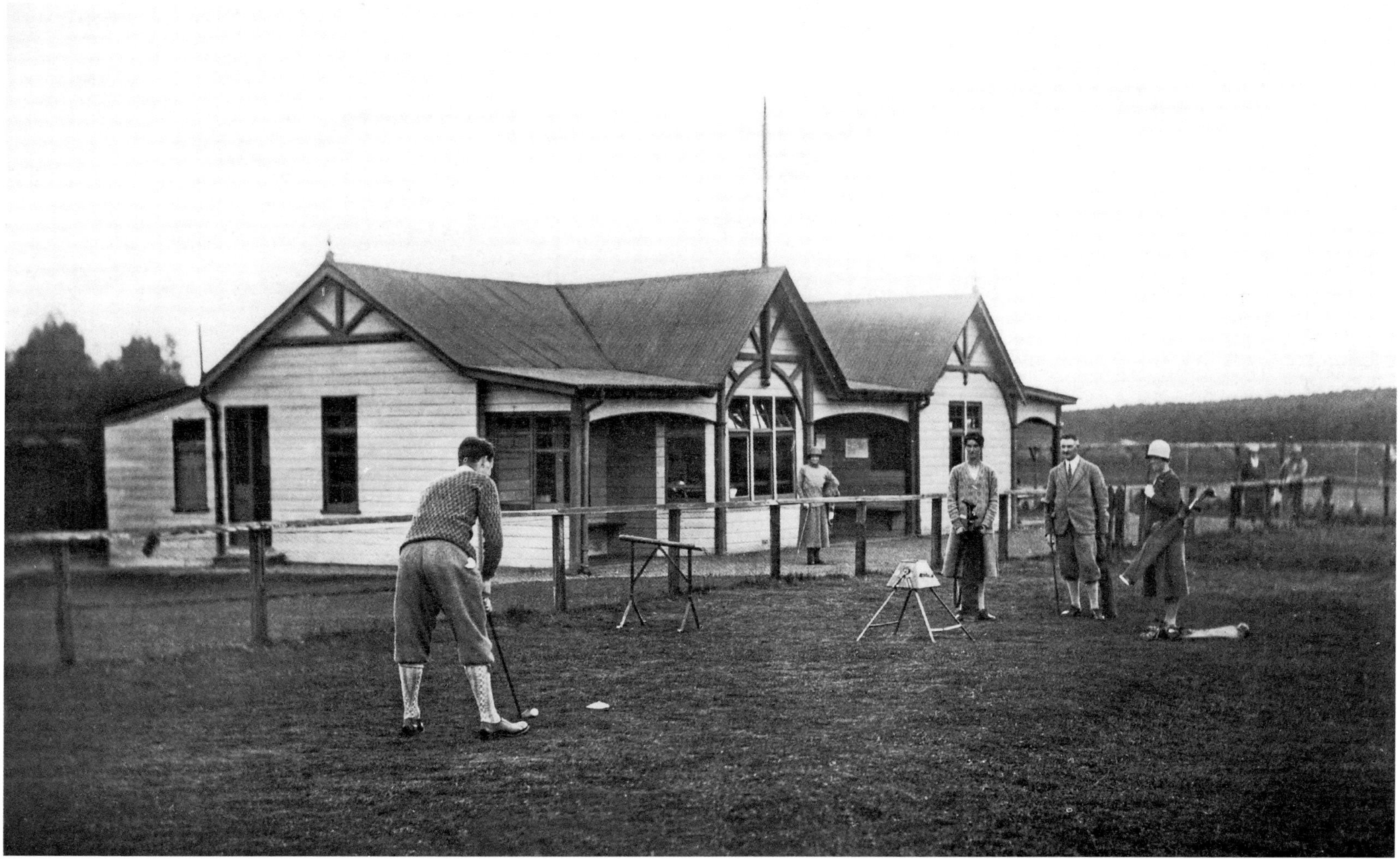

The golf course at Boat of Garten was an initiative by local people, especially railwaymen, who tamed rough pasture and broom bushes to create just six holes in 1898. With the railway bringing ever more visitors, modest extensions were made and a clubhouse built by 1910. Through visitor generosity, tennis courts were opened in 1921 and ambitions for an 18-hole golf course, designed by James Braid, five times Open champion, were fulfilled in 1932. Improvements to facilities and to the course have been ongoing and it is beautiful but sporting, with views to the high Cairngorms.

Photographed around 1908, Andrew M. Grant's shop continued a tradition as the hub of Boat of Garten until the Second World War (there is now another shop on the site). Adjacent is the public hall of 1896. Newspapers were delivered to 'The Boat' by train at an early hour. 'A.M.', pictured here, was enterprising, acting as a house-letting agent, renting out his villa 'Monaliath' and others in the district to summer visitors. In 1923 he built a bakery, tearoom and draper's shop but perhaps his greatest achievement was his management of the golf club's finances, which he did so carefully that the 18-hole course became a reality in 1932. He retired in 1939 and the shop now combines the local post office with other facilities.

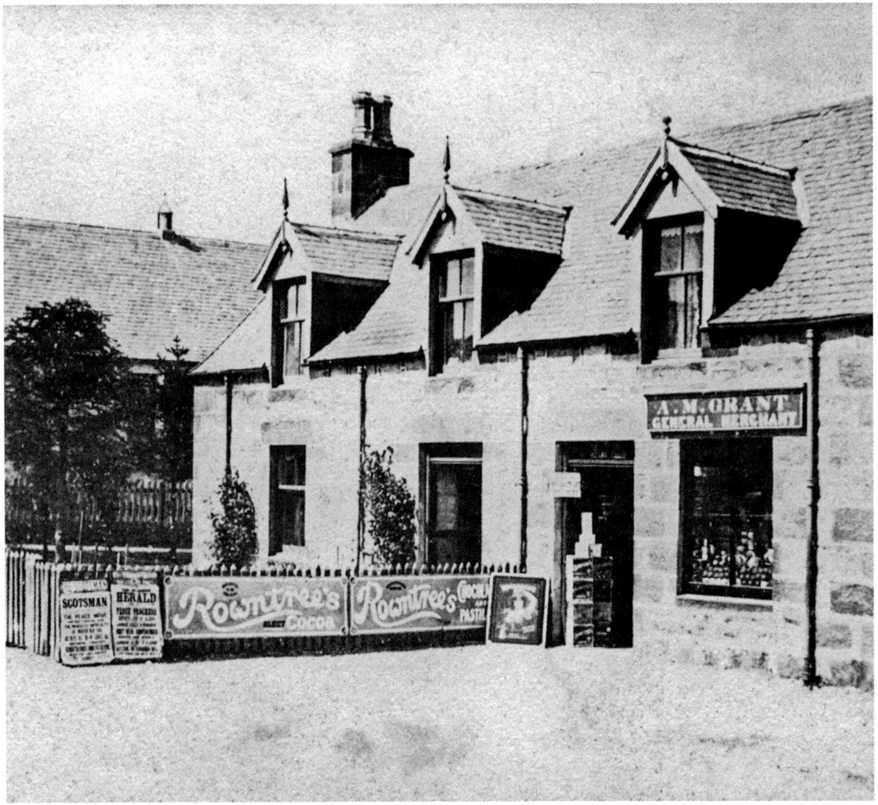


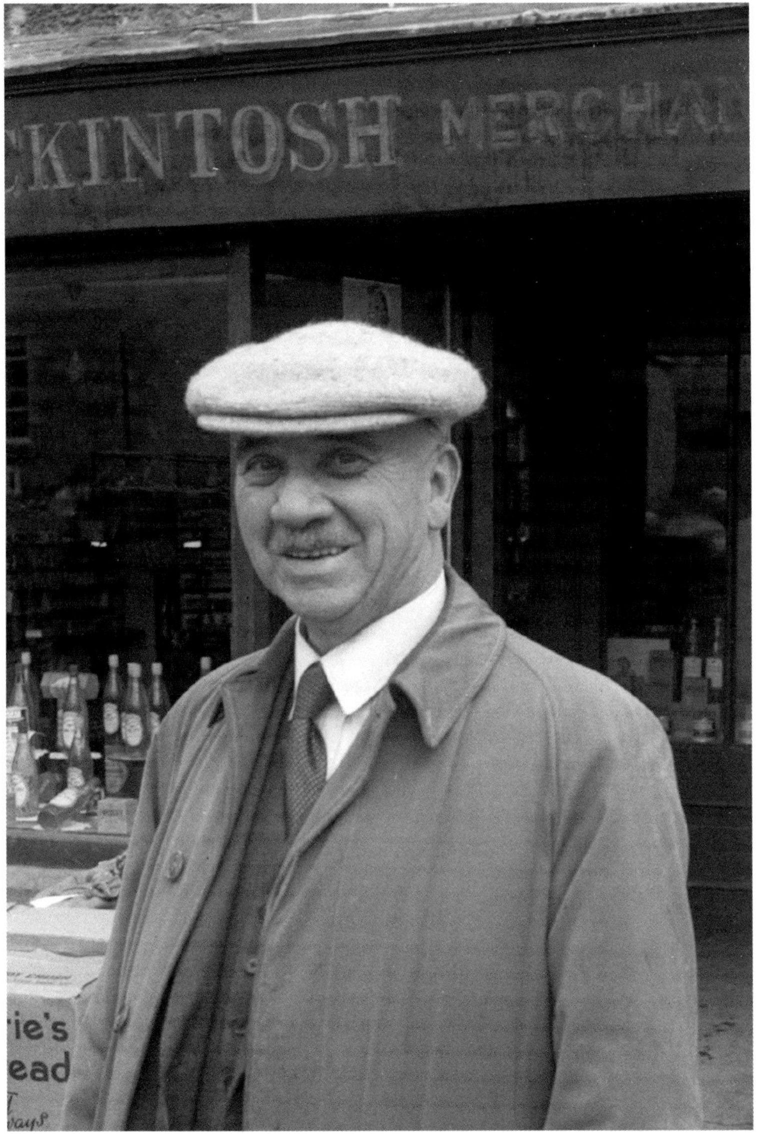

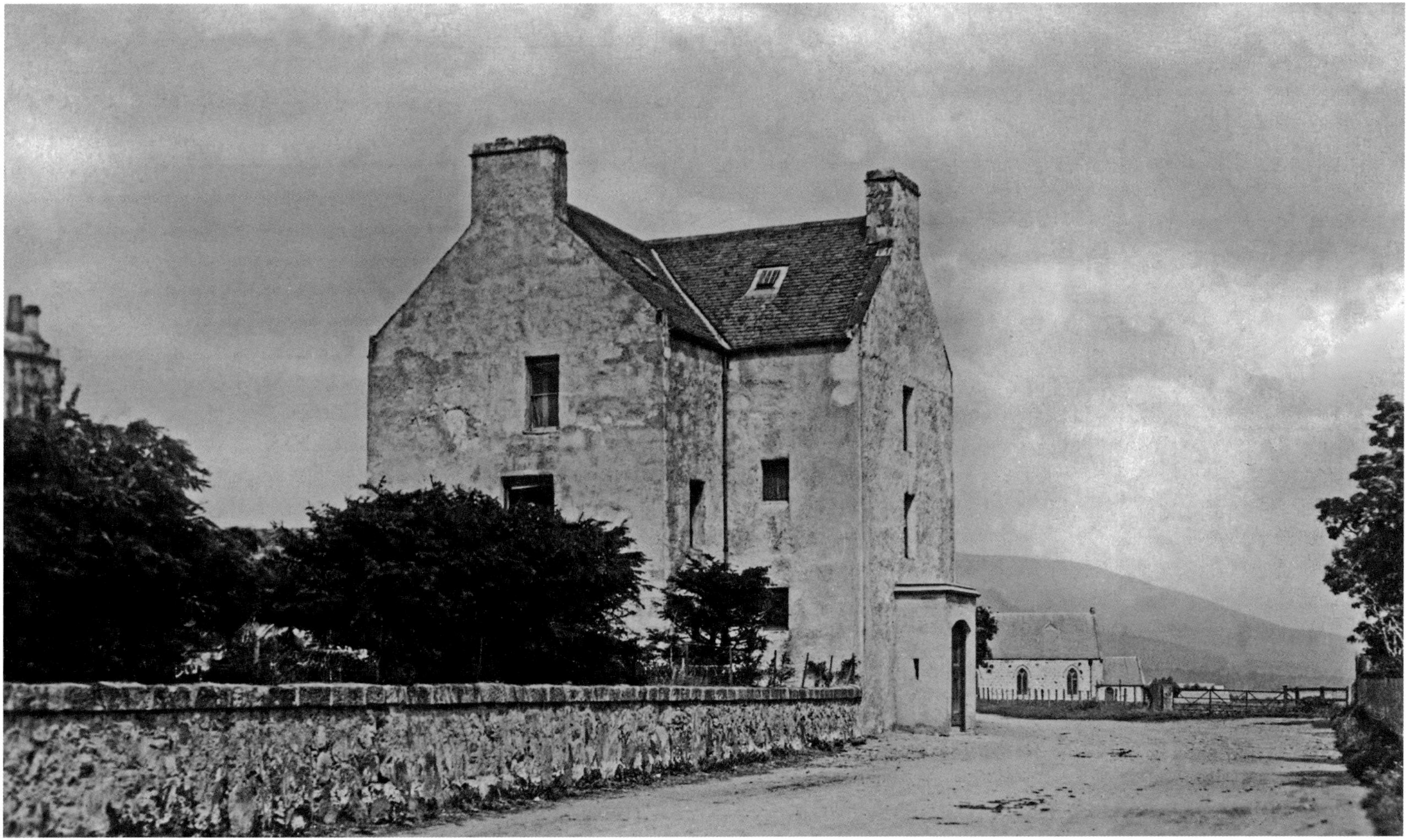

Dating from 1765, the Inn of Aviemore was an initiative by James Grant of Grant for the comfort of travellers on the King's Highway where a route joined from his castle. A fine house with farmland adjacent, the inn stood beside the Aviemore Burn where horses could be watered. In 1787 a distinguished guest was Robert Burns who was on a Highland tour. By the 1870s the inn was a shooting lodge, renamed Aviemore House. Subsequently owned by the Aviemore Station Hotel Company, it was first a guesthouse and latterly a farmhouse. In 1969 a road improvement, now seen as superfluous, caused this historic building to be demolished. To the right is the mission building of the Church of Scotland, later St Andrew's, erected in 1903.

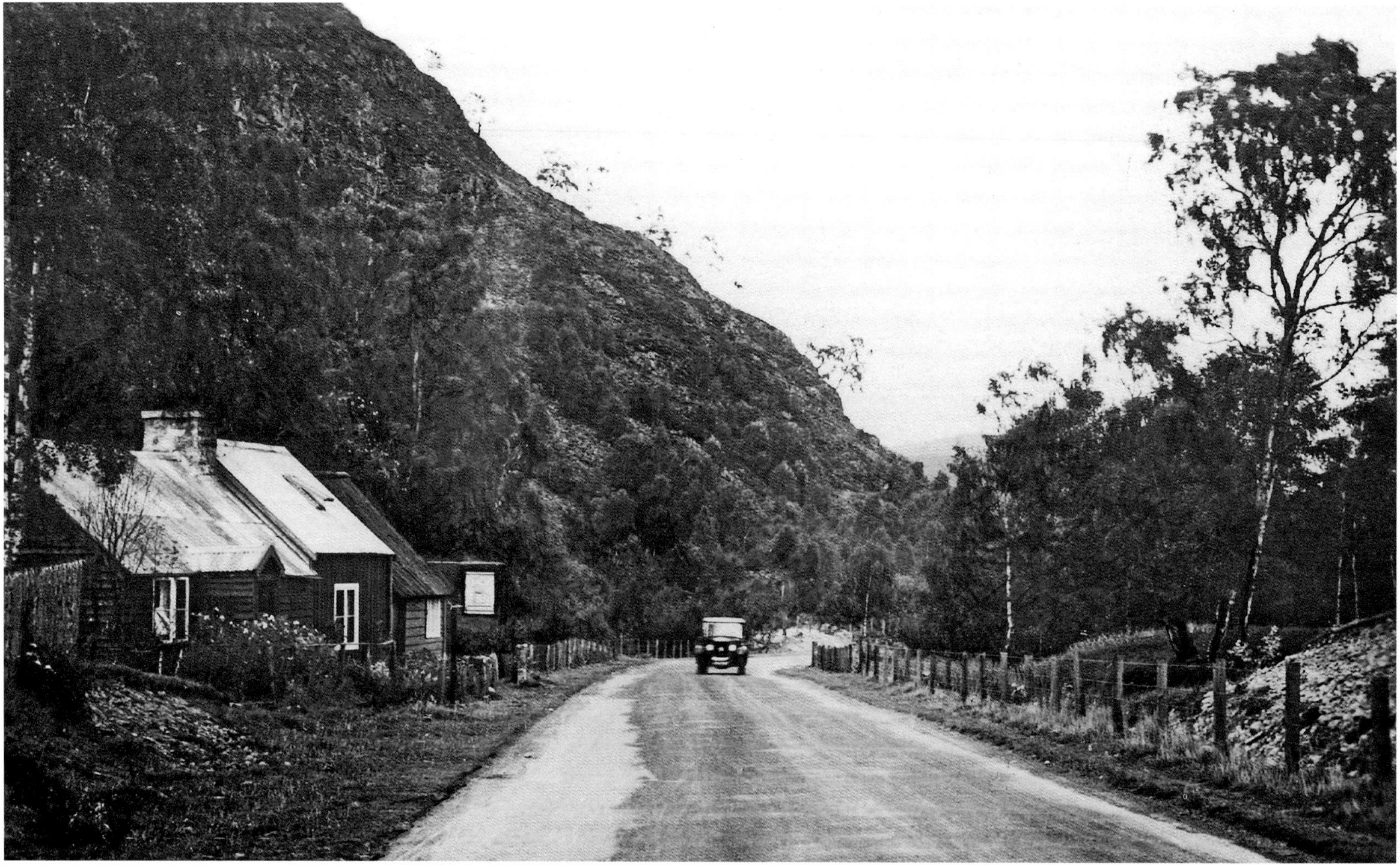

'Standfast Craigellachie' was the rallying cry of Clan Grant and the Rock of Craigellachie near Aviemore was their beacon hill in time of trouble. It was also traditionally seen as the southern limit of the clan's territory. (It should not be confused with the village of Craigellachie 25 miles to the north). Up to the 1950s the cottages on the left housed tearooms, known as 'The Tea Cup' and run by the Macdonald sisters, acknowledged to provide the best teas in the district. The Clarion Club for cyclists, set up in 1895 with socialist aims, encouraged its members to stop off here.

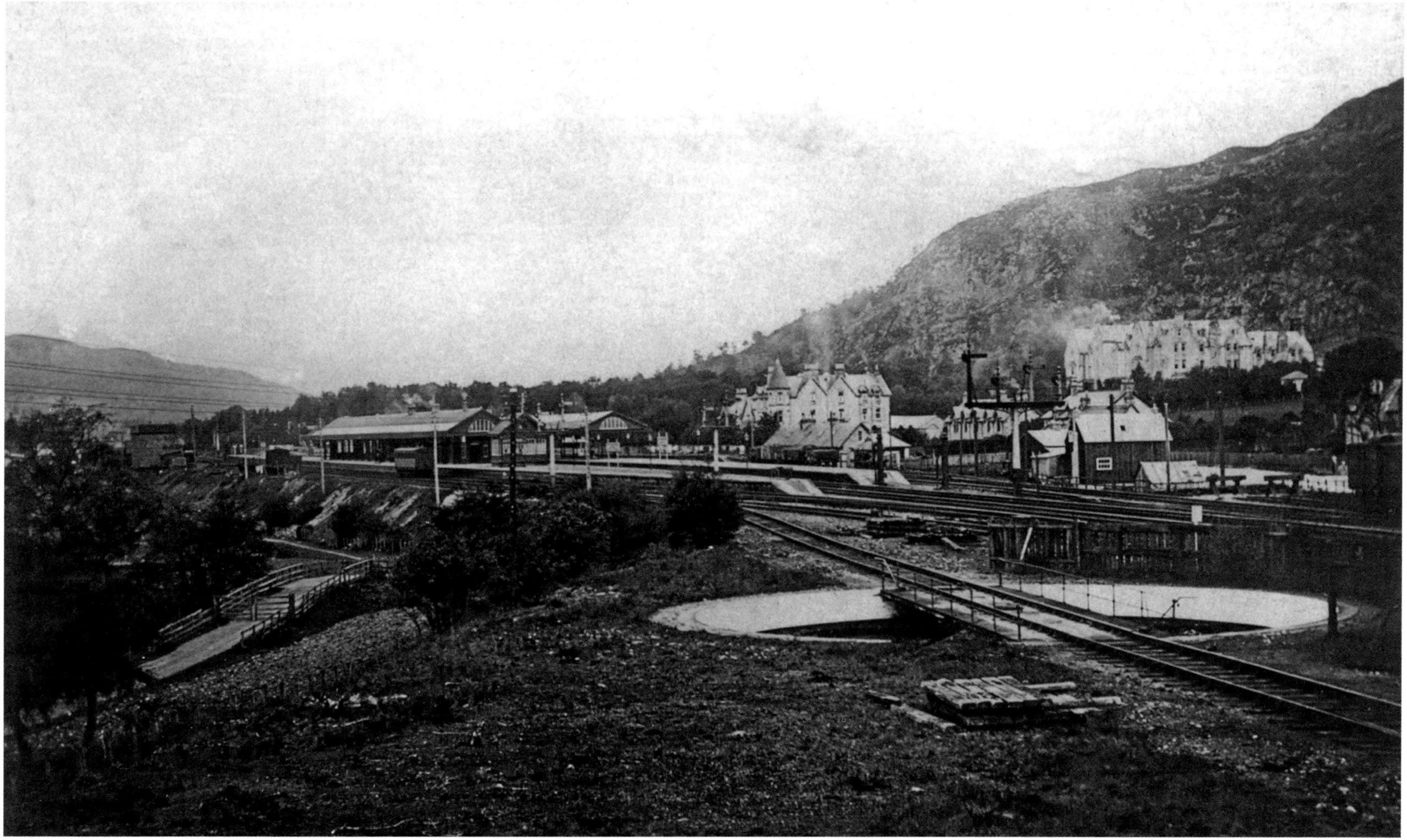

Looking south over the new Aviemore Junction in the early 1900s, this photograph shows this strategic location on the Highland Railway where the installations were largely constructed on ground created from material excavated from construction sites along the line. From the left, by the track to Dalfaber Farm, there is the water tower, then the station platforms with extensive verandas. In the foreground is a small turntable and numerous sidings, signal and telegraph posts. Far right is the imposing Station Hotel of 1899 and in the centre is the Cairngorm Private Hotel of 1903 (initially a Temperance establishment). The view also shows railway cottages, the stationmaster's villa, and various huts used for shops.

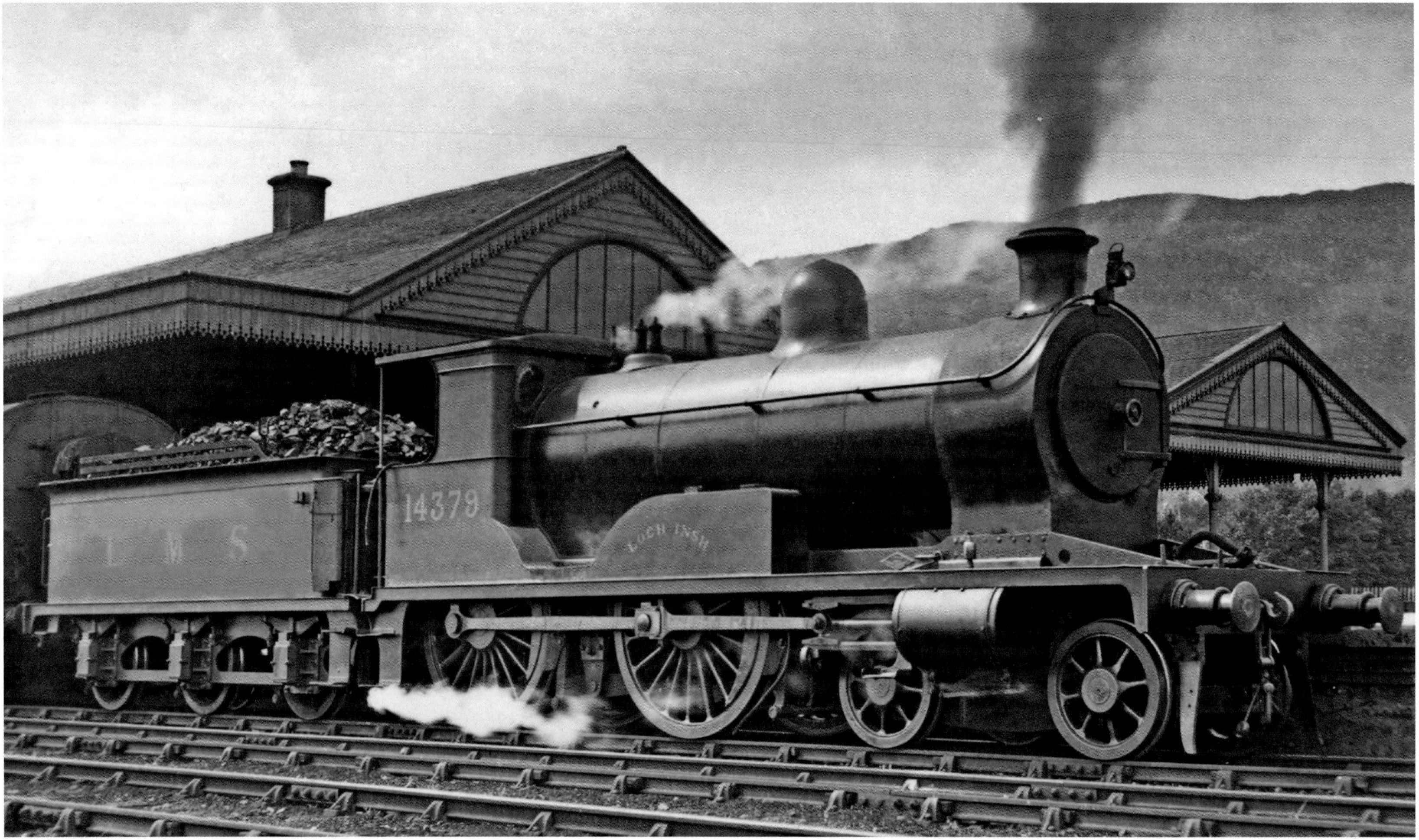


The locomotive *Loch Insh*, seen here with a train for Forres at Aviemore Junction in August 1937, was built by Dübs and Company in Glasgow in 1896 for the Highland Railway. The Loch class was designed by the HR's eminent Locomotive Superintendent David Jones for passenger traffic and eventually numbered 18 in total. They were well liked by staff. At the time of this photograph the engine was owned by the London, Midland & Scottish Railway (LMS). As No. 14379 it had been altered in appearance, the boiler, safety valves and chimney having been replaced. It survived into British Railways' years and was withdrawn in March 1948.

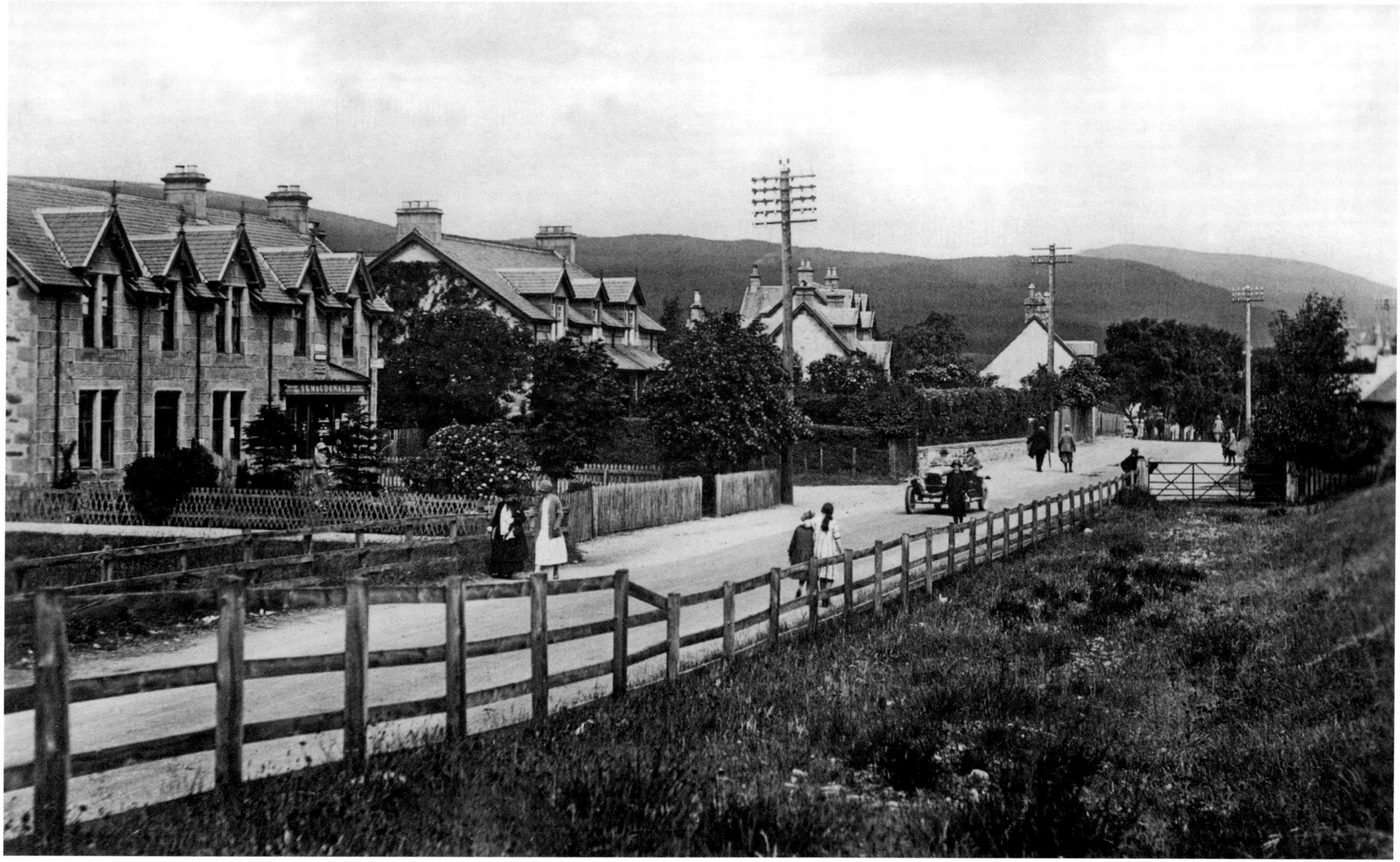

On the left of this 1920s photograph is Clune Villa, combining S.G. Macdonald's grocer and provision merchant's premises with the post office. Then comes Craiglea, then the home of the local GP, Dr Arthur C. Balfour. The stationmaster's house and the Telford tollhouse, the latter hard on the roadside, follow. Far right, Aviemore House can just be seen. This and the tollhouse were demolished in the 1960s for road improvements, and then two villas were removed in the 1990s to allow a supermarket to be constructed. Thus, the historic core of Aviemore was destroyed by lack of appreciation and negative planning.

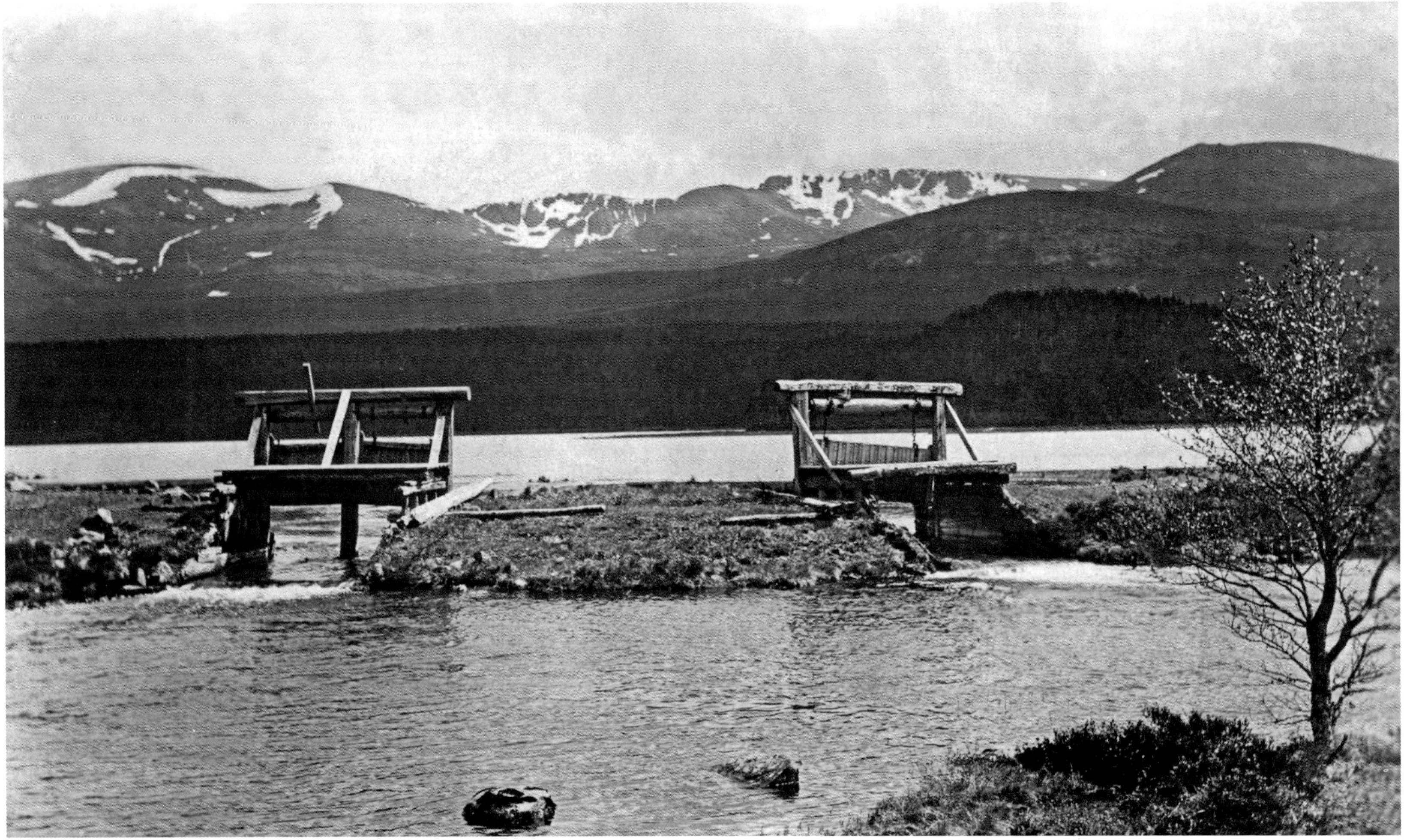

By the seventeenth century, timber was becoming scarce so the Highland pinewoods were targeted. Abernethy, Glenmore and Rothiemurchus forests had potential, although inaccessibility was a problem. The solution was to have men in currachs float logs out on the River Spey, a method later replaced by rafting the timber. Attempts were made to straighten tributaries and remove rocks while dams with sluices were constructed at the mouths of lochs. This installation at Loch Morlich raised its level and produced a good head of water for a spring float. The practice continued until the early 1900s when the railway had won the timber traffic.

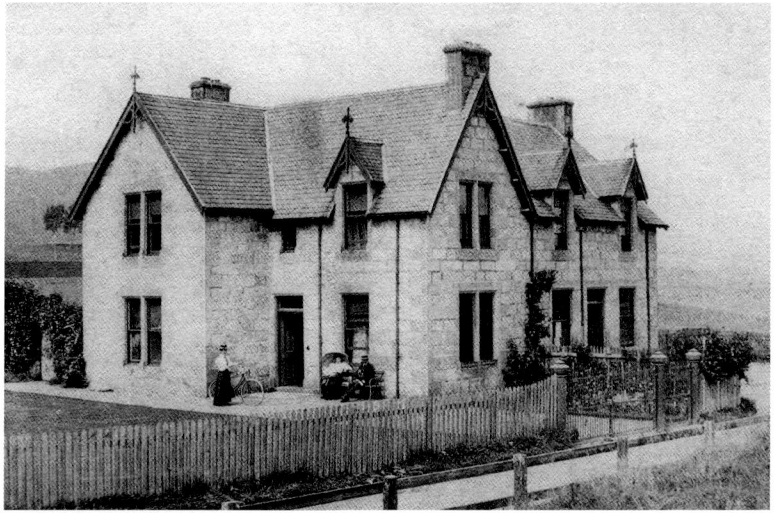

Aviemore Cottage was built by John Stott Lawrence, the first stationmaster in the village, who served there for 32 years. He was also a sub-postmaster and in the 1880s he transferred his post office and store from the east side of the railway to the west where a site had been chosen for Aviemore Cottage. This combined a village store with a new post office and letting accommodation. His wife and family then ran the business for him as railway employees were forbidden from doing so by the Highland Railway Company. This Victorian structure was demolished in 2000 and replaced by flats at Grampian Court.

Leaving Aviemore northbound on the Great Highland Road in the early 1900s, the cottage and steading at Muirton Farm are in the centre, while on the right old cottages and two newly built villas can seen. Among the buildings on the 'braes' is the Mill of Aviemore. Tenants were once 'thirled' – obliged to take their grain harvest to be ground at a single specific mill but this practice had been abandoned in Strathspey in the mid-eighteenth century. The farms and crofts had been set out in a reorganisation of land in the 1840s but the area has now been swallowed up in post-1960 housing developments as Aviemore has grown. The pine-clad hills on the Seafield estate are part of the Monadhliath Mountains.

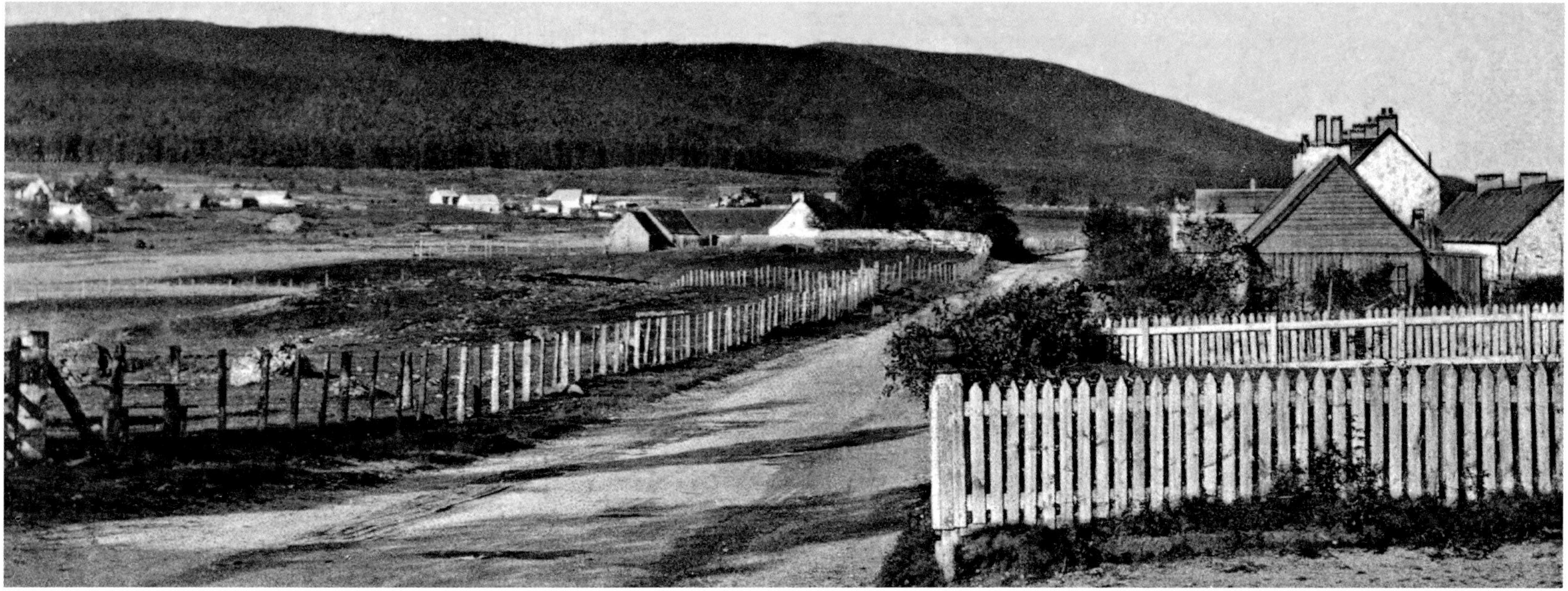

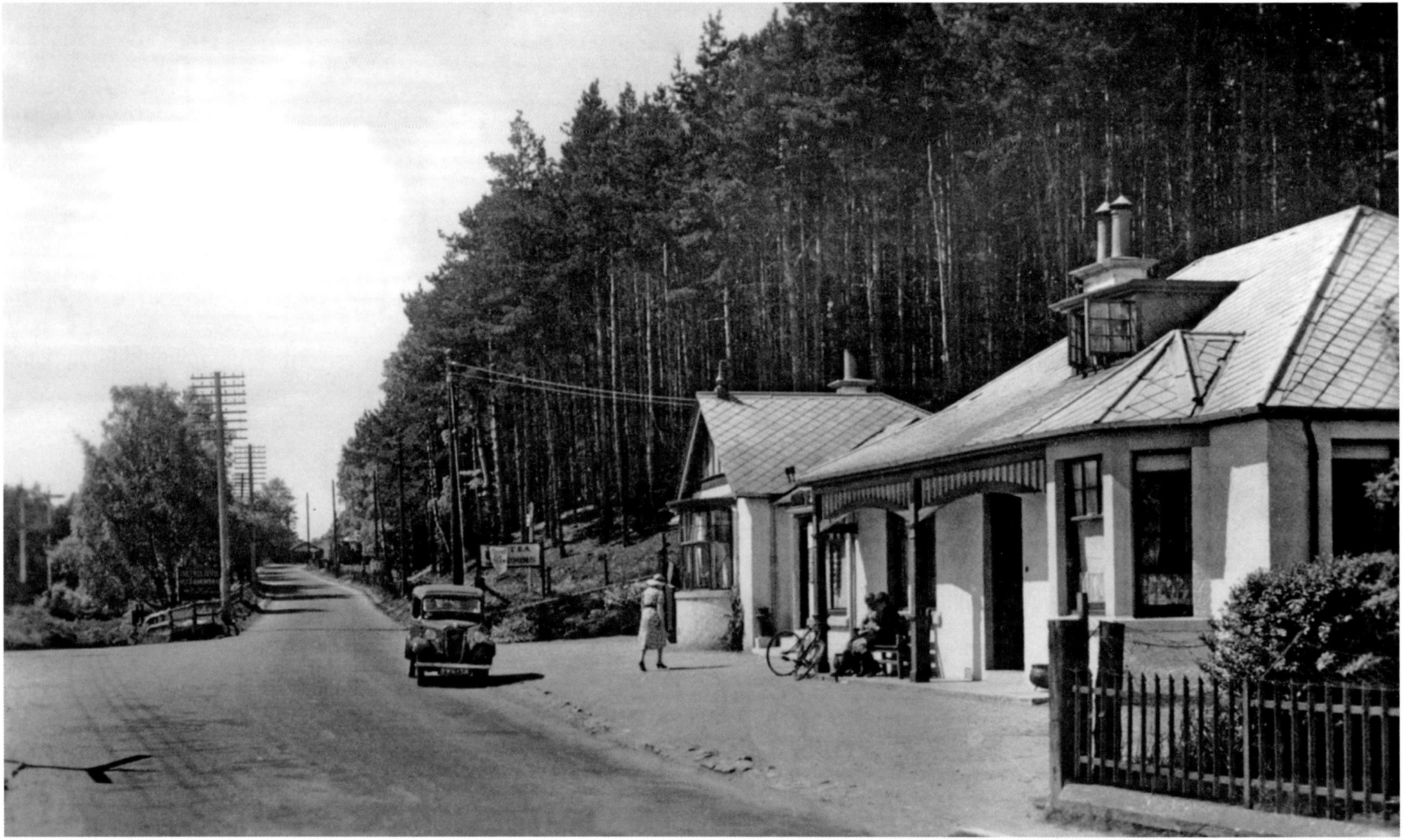

The Pot Luck Tearooms at the southern approach to Aviemore were established in the 1930s by a Mrs Lawrence who had married into the family of the enterprising first stationmaster in the village, J.S. Lawrence. Aviemore's development as a place with visitor appeal owed much to the family. The Pot Luck, built in bungalow style on the Great North Road, was famed for home baking and tapped into the new enthusiasm for motorcar touring and taking afternoon tea. It was also popular with young folk coming to the Scottish Youth Hostel which opened close by in 1933. The building now houses two restaurants and fast food outlets.

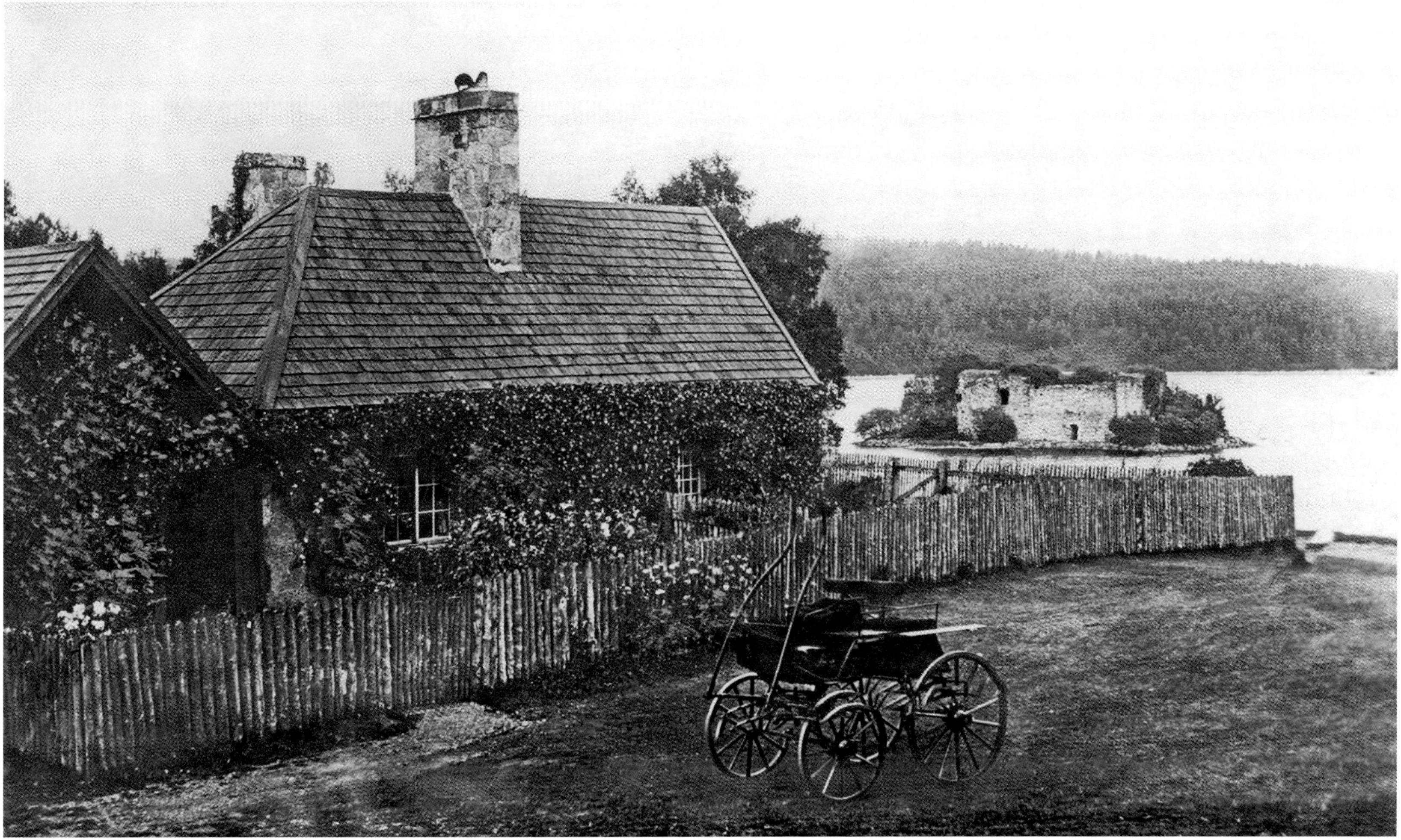

Loch an Eilein Castle is a ruined structure dating from the fourteenth century. In 1690 after the battle of Cromdale, the castle – a Rothiemurchus possession – was caught up in the Civil War when defeated Jacobites harried the chief and his family, who took refuge on the island and drove off the attackers. Rathad nam Mèirleach (the 'Thieves' Road'), associated with cattle rustlers, lies on the eastern shore of the loch. By the 1790s visitors were coming to view the castle and the ospreys nesting on it. The cottage, built around 1810, was designed by the laird and his children. In the 1830s the Duke of Bedford, a shooting lessee, had the path around the loch, including part of the Thieves' Road, improved to a carriage drive and today this is a visitor and nature trail.

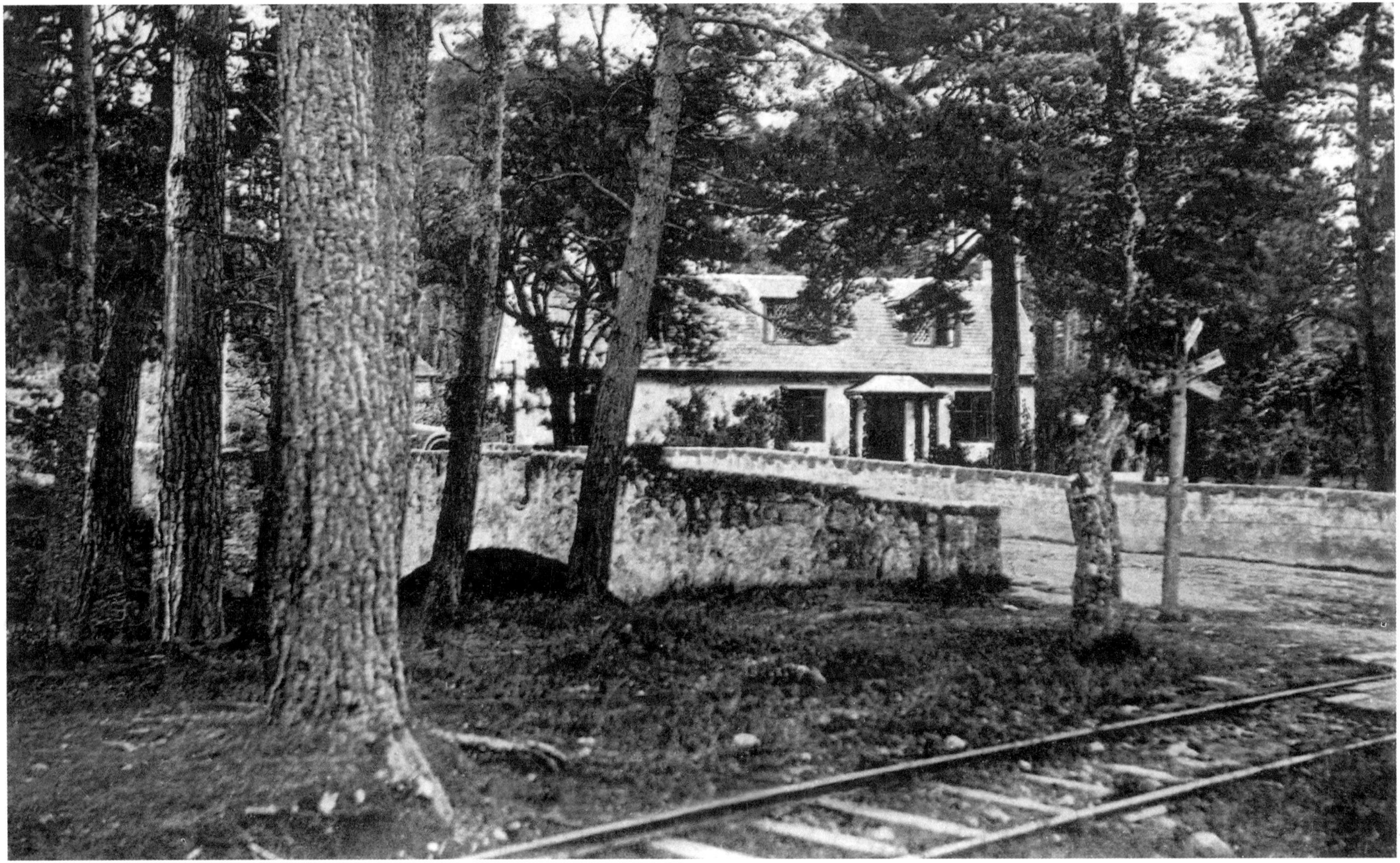

The old bridge at Coylum was built in the 1750s through the generosity of John Corrour Grant of Rothiemurchus who had made his money through military service. It stood at a rocky gorge close to the confluence of the Allt Beanaidh and the Luineag, which together form the River Druie. During the First World War, a 3 ft gauge railway with steam locomotives was installed by Canadian troops for hauling timber from Glenmore Forest via Rothiemurchus to a loading bank at Aviemore Station. The level crossing, seen here, was on the east side of the old bridge, which was replaced in 1969.